GOSH, MOM!
DON'T THEY KNOW
YOU'RE NOT ANYBODY?

GOSH, MOM!
DON'T THEY KNOW
YOU'RE NOT ANYBODY?

*One Woman's Journey through the Perils
of Performing, Living, Laughing, and Loving*

JUDY DYE

GOSH, MOM! DON'T THEY KNOW YOU'RE NOT ANYBODY?
ONE WOMAN'S JOURNEY THROUGH THE PERILS OF
PERFORMING, LIVING, LAUGHING, AND LOVING

iUniverse books may be ordered through booksellers or by contacting:

iUniverse
1663 Liberty Drive
Bloomington, IN 47403
www.iuniverse.com
1-800-Authors (1-800-288-4677)

ISBN: 978-1-5320-8407-2 (sc)
ISBN: 978-1-5320-8406-5 (e)

Library of Congress Control Number: 2019914659

Print information available on the last page.

iUniverse rev. date: 11/05/2019

INTRODUCTION

As the saying goes, "Life is a journey." My ongoing journey has been full of happiness, some heartache, and many surprises. I've been fortunate to have had these adventures, which I have the pleasure of sharing with you, the reader. I hope they will bring you a smile, a laugh, or a tear, and that you will enjoy these tales from a woman's journey.

PERFORMING
AND PERFORMERS

PERILS OF PERFORMING

As a professional singer, I've concertized in many different venues, including concert halls, such as the Kennedy Center; museums, including the National Gallery in Washington DC; and more unusual venues, such as Federal Hall, the Donnell Library, and Teddy Roosevelt's home in New York City. I've performed in colleges and universities and before large and small audiences; I've appeared on radio and television and in a jazz club. Performing on small cruise ships has proven a challenge when I had to maintain my balance while the ship rocked and the piano moved, to the great distress of my accompanist. I've demonstrated how the acoustics worked in an ancient Greek amphitheater in Turkey. I've sung for audiences of hundreds of children. But the greatest challenges have come at The Toledo Zoo's annual summer concert series, where I've appeared as soloist. These concerts are held in a five thousand-seat amphitheater. For starters, there was always only one rehearsal—very dicey when not only the music is rehearsed but the sound system and microphones have to be tried and checked and the position of the TV cameras arranged. In short, it could be total chaos. Then, during the performances there were the animals of the zoo, who sometimes tried to participate! Once my high notes set off loud squawking by the peacocks. Occasionally a lion would awaken and roar. Another time a trained bear, who performed with his trainer on the same program and was waiting backstage, decided to impatiently clang his chain against the bars of his enclosure while I was singing away. I tried to ignore his out-of-sync rhythm!

The most unforgettable concert was the one when a pigeon, roosting in the top of the huge proscenium arch, decided to do his business. Just as I ended my big aria, I felt an enormous splat on my shoulder. My first thought was that someone in the orchestra had thrown something at me; it felt like a smashed tomato! I whirled around, ready to accuse someone, saying, "Who threw some—" and then I saw my shoulder. There was no doubt what it was. It went down the entire length of my long yellow gown. By then the orchestra members were laughing, and the conductor came over and put his head on my clean shoulder, shaking with laughter. The audience thought he was so moved by my singing that he was overcome with emotion. Now I was laughing too, so I bowed to the orchestra and then to the audience, showing them my pigeon deposit. Of course, only the audience members in the first few rows could see it, but the word spread quickly, and soon all five thousand people were laughing. It was the first and last time I was literally laughed off the stage!

There were other memorable moments when I performed at the zoo. Back in the days when we didn't worry so much about security, after the concerts the soloist and the conductor would exit the stage door to a crowd of people, usually children and young people, seeking autographs. Once, my then-nine-year-old daughter was with me in the dressing room, and when we exited she was amazed at the crowd clamoring for my autograph. She came close to me and said, "Gosh, Mom! Don't they know you're not anybody?" That certainly put things into perspective!

LITTLE GOSPEL SINGER

My older daughter, opera singer Constance Hauman, has always loved to sing. I too, have always loved singing, so it was only natural that I taught her and my younger daughter many songs. They loved sitting at the piano, singing the songs they knew and loved, while pretending to play the piano, long before they'd had any lessons on that instrument.

When my girls were very young, I was the paid soprano at a large church. My husband, a doctor, was often on call, so the girls accompanied me to the rehearsals, where they filled many a coloring book while I sang with the choir and rehearsed my solos. On Sundays they went to the nursery Sunday school, where they learned children's church songs and stories from the bible.

One of my special friends was Charlotte Weiss, whom I met through a community choir and other musical organizations. Charlotte was also a singer, and we shared a love of opera. We often attended together the Metropolitan Opera productions that came to Detroit, Michigan. Not only did we share a love of music and art, we were both doctors' wives, so we shared the many inconveniences that came with that profession.

Charlotte had no children of her own, but she had a favorite young nephew, and when he came to visit we would get together to share activities with him and my girls. On one of these occasions

Charlotte invited Connie and me to join her and her nephew for lunch and a swim at her country club, whose membership was Jewish. Connie and I were both looking forward to that day, especially for the swim.

The day arrived, and when we had finished our lunch in the lovely dining room of the club, Charlotte said to Connie, "Your mother tells me that you like to sing. Would you sing something for me, please?"

Without hesitating, and certainly with no coaching from me, Connie threw back her little four-year-old head and belted out one of her favorites, "Jesus loves me, this I know; for the Bible tells me so. Little ones to him belong; they are weak but He is strong." At this point she was singing at the top of her voice, "Yes, Jesus loves me! Yes, Jesus loves me!"—I thought she would never stop— "Yes, Jesus loves me; the Bible tells me so."

Needless to say, the entire room of Jewish women, surprised to hear this song in these surroundings, turned to see from whom this unexpected Christian gospel was coming. There was much smiling and laughing, and I was so grateful that Charlotte said, "Thank you, Connie dear. That was lovely." Then Charlotte looked at me, and we both burst out laughing.

MOZART'S PIANO SYNDROME

I suffer from what I now know as Mozart's piano syndrome. I was stricken with this strange malady years ago, when I was an art and music docent at the Toledo Museum of Art. During that time, I traveled to Austria and saw several of the pianofortes and clavichords on which Mozart had played and composed, but the one in the apartment where he lived in Vienna left the greatest impression on me. It was so small, barely two and a half octaves, with a very soft, tinny sound. It seemed impossible that Mozart had played and composed his miraculous music on that puny instrument.

Part of the program I performed for children touring our museum included taking them up onto the stage of our magnificent concert hall, performing arias from operettas and operas, and talking about the composers of the music. Among the works was Despina's aria from Mozart's *Cosi Fan Tutte,* "*Una donna dei quindici anni*" ("A Woman of Fifteen Years"), which I sang in English. One day, as I was talking about Mozart and his genius, I started to describe that Viennese clavichord. I pointed out that Mozart never heard sounds like those we were hearing from the nine-foot Steinway concert grand, that Mozart heard only a tinny sound from a tiny piano. Suddenly, out of the blue, I was tearing up and could barely continue. After a few awkward moments, I composed myself, sang the aria, finished the program, and attributed my sudden emotion to my hormonal changes. However, in every subsequent program, if I started to talk about Mozart's piano, the tears would come! I soon realized I could not mention Mozart's piano in my presentations.

Unfortunately, this malady is still with me. If I talk about the many sound-enhancing, strange inventions that Beethoven experienced so painfully in a vain attempt to prevent his hearing loss, knowing that he never heard his music as we are privileged to hear it, Mozart's piano syndrome strikes me. If I try to speak about a particularly meaningful time, or if I receive an unexpected gift of appreciation, Mozart's piano syndrome takes me.

This syndrome has spread to other members of my family. My two sisters and my two daughters suffer from this same malady. When it strikes we can laugh at ourselves through our tears, but we've learned that there is no way to predict its onslaught, and there is no cure. So beware—this syndrome may strike you when you least expect it.

A CASUAL COMPLIMENT

When my daughters were young and living at home, they tolerated my practicing and teaching, which often took place after school hours. When I or my students began to sing, the doors to my daughters' rooms would slam, loudly. I was never certain whether they even listened to my singing.

One day when my younger daughter returned home from school, I was listening to a recording of one of my idols, Beverly Sills. As my daughter came into the room, she said, "Who was that singing?" When I answered her, she casually said, "You're as good as she is." Then she went up the stairs to her room and slammed the door. Without knowing it, she had given me the biggest compliment I could have received. Whether I ever sounded like one of the world's greatest singers or not, the fact that my young daughter thought I did moved me to tears of joy and gratitude.

BECOMING A LEGEND

One of my mother's lifetime friends was a woman named Hazel Moss (her married name). She had grown up with my mother and my aunt in the little village of Grahamville, Kentucky, just a few miles from Paducah, where the three of them had all come to live as married women. Hazel was an accomplished musician and, so it seemed to me, a jolly, gentle soul. She played both the piano and the organ, was a church organist for years, and had many students of organ and piano. My mother also played the piano, and at one time we had a Hammond organ as well. My mother and Hazel would often play duets, one at the piano and the other at the organ, taking turns. Hazel taught me to play a few pieces on our Hammond organ, and she showed me how to move my feet on the pedals in a more efficient manner.

Hazel's musicianship was impressive, as was her size. While I was growing up, Hazel seemed to grow larger and larger. She and her husband, Aubin, loved to eat, especially sweets. Hazel was a superb baker, so cakes, pies, bread, and cookies, along with homemade ice cream, were staples of their diet. They had no children, so they often joined my family or my Aunt Weda's family for suppers and holiday dinners, where they indulged in their favorite activity, consuming large portions. Hazel continued to expand to the point that she eventually needed a wheelchair in order to move around.

Surprisingly, her feet remained relatively small, but her ankles were so fat that they hung over the tops of her shoes.

By the time I was an adult, with children of my own, Hazel's size had become a legend in our family, much like Rabelais's Gargantua! We might see a very obese person and say, "Oh my, he (or she) is bigger than Hazel Moss!" or conversely, "He (or she) is not as big as Hazel Moss!"

Adults should always pay attention to what children overhear them say. In my career I had the privilege of being acquainted with the renowned Greek pianist Gina Bachauer, having appeared in the same music festival as she did. Later that same year she appeared in concert in Toledo, my hometown, and I took my two young daughters to hear her performance. After the concert, we went backstage so they could meet her and get her autograph. Gina Bachauer was a lovely, very heavy older woman, so heavy that her ankles hung over the tops of her shoes. My younger daughter, then about five years old, noticed this, and asked in a much-too-loud voice, "Is she as big as Hazel Moss?" Oh, the legends we create! I quickly shushed my daughter, giving her a look to silence her, as she whispered, "Well, is she?" Fortunately Ms. Bachauer didn't see or hear this little drama, and when I introduced her to my daughters, she smiled sweetly at them and graciously autographed their programs. She did not know that she was not nearly as legendary as Hazel Moss!

SAVING STRAVINSKY

My good friend Louise, a very gifted pianist, studied for her master's degree in piano under Soulima Stravinsky, at the University of Illinois. Soulima's wife, Francoise, was a lovely little Frenchwoman, and she and Louise became friends. Many years later, while attending the Sarasota Opera, I discovered that Francoise was a patroness of one of the productions of a French opera, and her picture was in the program. The following year, again at the Sarasota Opera, I saw Francoise, introduced myself as Louise's friend, and we had a lovely conversation. She was a tiny, fragile lady in her nineties by then. She not only remembered Louise but remembered exactly what Louise had performed on her master's recital back in 1960!

Later that same evening, at intermission, I was in the always interminably long line for the ladies' room, and I noticed that Francoise was about five places in front of me. Just as I actually entered the ladies' room, I saw Francoise enter a stall. After a few minutes, I heard her knocking on the stall door and calling, "*Au secours, au secours!*" (Help, help!).

No one seemed to notice, so I left my coveted place in line and went to her stall, saying, "*Qu'est ce qu'il y a, Madame?*" (What is it, Madame?)

"*Je ne peux pas l'ouvrir! Je ne peux pas l'ouvrir!*" (I can't open it! I can't open it!) came the answer.

Our conversation continued in French. She was trying to push the lock, and I was telling her to pull it and slide it to the right. "*Tirez et glissez-la a la droite.*"

"*Je ne peux pas, je ne peux pas! Au secours, au secours!*"

At that point, all the ladies in the restroom were saying, "What should we do"? There was only one solution. I dropped to my knees and then to my stomach, and in my long black dress I belly-crawled under the door of the stall. I then slowly stood up inside next to Francoise, who clapped her little hands and said, "*Oh, merveilleux, merveilleux!*" I opened the door to the stall, and out she walked proudly, smiling, to the applause of the ladies watching the rescue. To my great surprise my black dress wasn't even dirty—but my heroism didn't advance my place in line!

CHARMED BY DRACULA

Janos Starker, the great Hungarian cellist, was practicing in my living room! I wanted to be in that room with him, but I had to be content in the kitchen, being as quiet as possible, keeping my dogs from barking, and taking the phone off the hook—but savoring every note I heard.

Starker was in Toledo to perform with the Toledo Symphony Orchestra, and he needed a space in which to practice. It had to be spacious, have a piano, and be a place where no one would disturb him or know his whereabouts. The conductor of the Toledo Symphony, Serge Fournier, was a friend of our family, and he asked if I would allow Starker to use our large living room. "Allow him? I would be honored!" I responded.

"But you must not interrupt him once he begins rehearsing," I was warned. I agreed, although I was eagerly awaiting a chance to talk with him.

I was also to provide him with an ashtray and not object to his smoking, which was difficult for me; I have always been opposed to smoking, especially in my home! I knew that Starker was a chain smoker; he was known to have cancelled a performance when he was forbidden to have his preconcert cigarette backstage! I couldn't risk him cancelling his appearances with our symphony because I wouldn't let him smoke! I also knew that he was a prodigious drinker of Scotch, starting early in the day, and I hoped I wouldn't have to provide him with that beverage. Happily, I did not.

At the appointed hour in the early afternoon, Starker was delivered to my door. I had seen pictures of him but was surprised at the severity of his countenance. With his heavy eyebrows, cleft chin, dark, penetrating eyes, mostly bald head, and angular face, he could have played the role of Count Dracula had he been wearing a cape! Once inside the house, he became utterly charming, graciously thanking me for giving him this "private" time. He took his cello out of its case, sat by the piano, lit a cigarette, and began his practicing. I then disappeared into the kitchen, which was difficult for me, because I wanted to ask him so many questions about his life. I had read that he'd been born in Budapest, that he'd received his first cello at age six, that he'd been teaching others at age eight and had had five students at age twelve! He'd made his professional debut at age fourteen—with a three-hour notice! He'd become a well-known cellist at a young age, and a meeting with Pablo Casals had propelled him into his career. I had read about many members of his family being lost in the Holocaust—including his brothers, who were sent to a forced labor camp and later murdered by the Nazis—and that he had spent three months in a labor camp. He'd made his way to Paris after World War II and come to the United States in 1948. I wanted to ask him about his extensive teaching career. I had so many questions that had to wait!

When I sensed he was ending his practicing, I ventured timidly to the living room. He looked up, smiled, and invited me to come in and chat, while he had his after-practice cigarette. We had a lovely visit, with no serious conversation or questions. He told me where he preferred to vacation—on Isla de las Mujeres, just off the coast of Mexico near Cancun, and we swapped travel stories. During our chat, Mrs. Starker arrived with M. Fournier to escort him back to his hotel. She was a striking brunette, what one calls a "handsome" woman, with beautiful features. Everyone thanked me again for my hospitality, when it was I who was thankful for this rare occasion.

Now Starker's Draculean countenance had disappeared, and I was totally captivated by this charming, exquisite musician, whose rich cello sounds had echoed through my house and into my head and heart.

When I close my eyes, I can still see and hear Janos Starker playing his beautiful cello in my living room.

Janos Starker died in 2013 at the age of eighty-eight.

CAESAR'S QUESTION

"Et tu, Bruta?" These words were spoken to me by Josef Blatt, and I've never forgotten them. As a graduate student in vocal performance at the University of Michigan, I had the good fortune of appearing in five of Mr. Blatt's opera productions: as Zerlina in *Don Giovanni*, Norina in *Don Pasquale*, Gilda in *Rigoletto*, Despina in *Cosi Fan Tutte*, and Freia in *Das Rheingold*. Though short of stature, Mr. Blatt had a commanding presence and an encyclopedic knowledge of every detail of each opera. His coaching and rehearsals were taxing, joyous, and inspiring. He praised my work, and I thrived under his encouragement.

Josef Blatt was born in Vienna, studied piano at the age of three, and was considered a child prodigy. He chose conducting for his career, which began in Czechoslovakia and then returned him to Vienna in 1933, as director of the opera school of the Vienna Conservatory of Music. In 1937, driven out by the Nazis, Josef and his wife, Renee, fled Austria for the United States. They arrived speaking no English, but Josef taught himself that language by listening to the radio and reading detective stories. Soon he was guest-conducting the New York Philharmonic, and he later joined the conducting staff of the Metropolitan Opera. From the Met, at the recommendation of Eugene Ormandy, Mr. Blatt came to the University of Michigan to establish an opera program and a symphony orchestra. Both programs became among the most outstanding in the country, no longer considered collegiate but professional in their quality of performance. At Michigan, he produced over seventy opera productions, thirty-two for which he made the English translations. All of his opera productions and symphony concerts were conducted entirely by memory.

There was one summer when I happened to be living near the Blatt family, and I often gave Mr. Blatt a ride to the campus. He hated driving and was a terrible driver. Since I lived nearby and had a car, he asked me for a lift. I happily obliged, and it became an almost daily occurrence. Our rides together were filled with conversations about music, life, careers, choices, history, and families. All were animated and interesting. We became friends, and I was often invited to his home to have dinner with his family. I was very honored. Mr. Blatt came to trust me and count on me, not only to deliver him safely to the campus but also to be well prepared and to know my part.

Besides the operas, I also studied German lieder in a class taught by Blatt, as we students called him. He seemed to know from memory every song by Schubert, Schumann, Brahms, Wolf, and Strauss. I loved that class and always tried to live up to his expectations, to be prepared and to win his praise.

One day, as each member of the class performed his or her assigned song, each one made a mistake of some sort, either musical or of pronunciation or interpretation. When it was my turn, I, who was always prepared, also made a mistake. I seem to remember it was a rhythmical error. Blatt looked at me with his big, sad, blue eyes, made larger by his thick glasses, and said, "Et tu, Bruta?" I'll never forget those words or the look of disappointment in his eyes. I'm happy to say he did forgive me, and I vowed to never make a mistake again in his lieder class.

In recent political times, which have elicited disappointment and unexpected betrayal, I've often silently asked that question, purportedly posed by Julius Caesar and made immortal by William Shakespeare, albeit in a different declension. I would make it plural: "Et vos, Brutae et Brutii?"

A GRAND SURPRISE WITH
MICHEL LEGRAND

One Sunday night in 1978, around nine thirty, our household was doing its usual Sunday night activities. My daughters were upstairs finishing their homework for school the next day and would soon be getting ready for bed. My husband was in his study, preparing a paper he was to present at a medical conference, and I was in the living room at the piano, working on my repertoire for an upcoming recital. Suddenly our front doorbell rang. I couldn't imagine who would be calling on us at that hour, unannounced, on a Sunday evening. I went to the door, looked through its window, and was surprised to see Serge Fournier, our conductor friend, with a clarinet player from the symphony, also a friend, and a third man, who at first glance I didn't recognize. But then I was shocked to realize it was Michel Legrand! When I opened the door, Serge stepped in and announced that Michel needed a piano immediately. The three of them had been partying, and Michel had a melody in his head that he needed to play. Serge, as our friend, had been to our house often, and he knew that I had a grand piano and a very large living room. They had been at a restaurant not far from our neighborhood, so Serge had thought nothing of popping in unannounced. Of course I was delighted to see them, and especially to meet Michel Legrand, who was in the area to perform with the Detroit Symphony and the

Toledo Symphony. Michel and Serge were old friends. They were the same age, in their late forties, had attended and graduated from the Paris Conservatoire together, and were having a wonderful time joking and being school "boys" again.

I summoned my girls and husband to join us in the living room. After introductions all around, Michel sat down at the piano and started to play, working on his new tune and playing others.

My older daughter, Connie, had recently played the part of Maria in her high school's production of *West Side Story*, and Serge had attended one of her performances. He was quite impressed with her singing, so now he asked her to sing for Michel. She chose "I Feel Pretty," and Michel accompanied her. He, too, was impressed and complimentary of her singing, and we were all thrilled. *Now*, I thought, *Serge will ask me to sing*, since I had appeared as soloist with the Toledo Symphony several times—but he didn't! Nor did Michel, and I was too intimidated to suggest it. After he left I could have kicked myself for not being more assertive. But it was an evening to remember, with much laughter and joking.

Before the evening ended, Michel expressed a desire to visit the Toledo Museum of Art, and now I did assert myself. Since I was an art and music docent at our museum, I offered to arrange a tour and be the guide for him and his wife. She had not accompanied him to our house, but she would join us for the museum tour.

Monday morning early I phoned the museum, which is always closed on Mondays, and arranged with the staff woman who was in charge of the docents to let us come for a private tour. When I told her for whom the tour would be, she volunteered to be the guide, so once again my thunder was stolen! Thus it was that on Monday afternoon, Serge, Michel, his wife, and I met the docent leader for a tour like no other. She was a prim, proper, serious young woman who had once been a nun. I was a little nervous, because on the way to the museum Serge and Michel had been joking and laughing, in French, of course, and their jokes had been somewhat ribald, to say the least. When our tour began, all scholarly and serious, it wasn't long before the "schoolboys" Serge and Michel cut loose with their irreverent, ribald, and funny comments, in English, for our guide's enjoyment. Soon, and in spite of herself, she was laughing with them. It was fortunate that we were having a private tour, because the museum walls were ringing with hilarity before the tour was finished. Michel praised our guide to the point that she was blushing and smiling, looking like a schoolgirl herself. It was truly a memorable museum experience.

Michel Legrand has composed hundreds of songs and film scores, won Oscars, written an opera, conducted symphony orchestras, played and composed jazz, soloed as a pianist, and recorded as a singer. He has explored every possible musical venue, and he is quoted as saying that to him music is life.

I will always regret not having taken the opportunity to sing for and with him, but I am still thrilled at the memory of my Michel Legrand encounter.

Michel Legrand died January 26, 2019.

TRAVEL

TRAIN TRAVELS IN ITALY

In the 1970s, when my two daughters were ages twelve and ten, my husband and I took them on a trip to Italy and France. It was quite an adventure, with a few mishaps, thanks to misunderstood translation of certain words. We were in Venice and were taking a train to Monaco, in Monte Carlo, the city-state surrounded by France. My husband had purchased the tickets at the train station in Venice, and as we searched for the correct track with the correct train, I would ask: "*E treno per Monaco?*" and "*E binario per treno per Monaco?*" and would receive a *Si, si, Signora*, with a finger pointing to the track and the train. We boarded, found our reserved seats, and made ourselves comfortable. I considered myself a seasoned traveler, having lived in France and traveled extensively when I was in college. I insisted that we had to carry our own luggage. My little girls each had very lightweight, plaid cloth suitcases, and they knew the rule: you carry your own, no exceptions. As the train pulled out of the Venice station, I noticed that it seemed to be going in the same direction as when we'd arrived from Milan, but my husband pointed out that probably it had to go north a little way before it turned to head toward France. *Hmm.* We then went into the dining car, and I noticed that the bread in the bread baskets was dark brown—not very Italian or French looking. Next we heard announcements being made over the intercoms, and they were first spoken in German, then Italian, and lastly in French. I was beginning to suspect that we were not heading to France. When the dining car attendant appeared, I asked him, "*E treno per Monaco?*"

"*Si, Signora,*" he replied. A little later I repeated that question and received another "*Si, si, Signora.*"

We were given a menu. The large print was in German, followed by Italian, and French in small print. So I nervously asked, "*E treno per Monaco in Francia?*"

"*No, signora, Monaco in Allemagna.*"

"Oh no! We're on the wrong train, heading for Germany!"

"*Ma, Signora, non e problema?*"

"*Si, si, e gran problema!*"

The conductor was summoned, and I explained to him it was indeed a "gran problema." He told me that Monaco in Italian means Munich! My husband had bought tickets from the booth that said Monaco—neither of us knew it meant Munich! The conductor, in broken English, explained that the train would stop briefly in Verona, that we would have a few minutes to get tickets for the next train that was headed to Nice and Monaco. The train had barely stopped, and off we flew into the Verona station, my girls with eyes big as saucers, carrying their little bags. I rushed up to the window for tickets, where it said in English, "Here we only speak Italian"! I couldn't make myself understood in my operatic Italian, so I tried French, and that worked. The next train would be there in five minutes, and we would have two minutes to get on board. The train came, hardly stopping before starting up again, and my little troupers jumped aboard without a whimper, as I broke the rule and helped them throw their bags on. We were all out of breath but happy to be on what we hoped was the correct train. When I asked: "*E treno per Monaco in Francia?*" It was a great relief to hear "*Oui, oui, Madame, c'est le train pour Monaco en France.*"

More adventures.

Earlier on our trip, when we were in Rome, we had another mishap, which was entirely my fault. I insisted we take the bus whenever possible, and after a full day of sightseeing, I saw we were at a stop where the bus would take us back to the vicinity of our hotel. When the bus arrived, it was very crowded. The doors opened at the front of the bus, I pushed my ten-year-old daughter into the bus, and to my horror the doors closed and the bus took off. I saw my daughter looking panic-stricken through the glass panels of the doors. I started running as fast as I could, yelling and screaming, "Stop! You have my daughter, you have my daughter!" and waving my arms like a maniac. My husband and my other daughter were running behind me. Finally the bus driver saw me in his side mirror and stopped the bus. The doors opened, and I pulled my daughter off the bus as the driver yelled at me in Italian, words I didn't understand. But his gestures let me know that I had done a stupid thing. "*Signora molta stupida!*" One boards a bus in the back and exits the front, something I had inconveniently forgotten! It was such a frightening experience that I decided taxis would be our mode of transportation after that, to the great relief of my family!

And still more.

My then ten-year-old daughter has always been resourceful. On this same trip, while in Italy, most of the toilet tissue we encountered was like little squares of waxed paper—not very absorbent or comfortable to use. At one of the restaurants in Florence where we dined, this daughter excused herself to visit the ladies' room. She was gone for such a long time that I headed that way to find what was keeping her. I met her coming back in our direction, and she was smiling like the cat that had swallowed the canary. She was wearing a two-piece dress, with the top coming over her waist like a peplum. She came close to me and lifted her top. She had found "real" toilet paper in that ladies' room, and had wound it around and around and around her waist, giving us a generous supply for the next few days! I had been ready to reprimand her for being in the restroom for so long, but instead I gave her a big hug and kiss. She was taking care of her family.

AIRPORT FUN

When my husband and I first started dating we lived in different cities, so sometimes I would fly to him, and sometimes he would fly to Toledo, where I lived. Back and forth, we always met in airports. At one point I decided to meet him in costume. I owned a genuine pith helmet, so I donned it, along with khaki shirt, khaki shorts, hiking boots, and enormous sunglasses, with wipers on them like windshield wipers. I held a sign that read, "Welcome N. M. Dye, mighty mogul" and waited for him to arrive. He didn't recognize me immediately, but by the time he reached the bottom of the escalator, he knew it was me. I could see him laughing, pleasantly surprised and amused. Thus began our disguising ourselves, or trying to, for many times afterward.

There was the time I wore a camp counselor outfit, with a large whistle around my neck and a shirt emblazoned Camp Wausau. This was because, on my first visit to Wausau, Wisconsin, where Nick had recently moved, we had played tennis, done a round of golf, climbed a mountain, and gone canoeing, biking, and swimming—just like at camp. Other people who were boarding the plane to Wausau asked me, "Where is Camp Wausau? We live near there, and we've never heard of it."

Another time Nick was sitting in the airport waiting room in a wig and nose, looking like Chico Marx. He was sure no one would recognize him, but a former colleague, whom I didn't know and who reached the waiting room before I did, walked right up to him and asked, "Nick, is that you?" Nick was so disappointed that his disguise didn't work.

During the holidays when I flew to Wausau, I wore a rubber Mrs. Santa Claus face mask, which I put on just before exiting the plane. Several little children saw me and shouted, "Look! There's Mrs. Santa!" It didn't take long for Nick to spot me, thank goodness, because I was perspiring like crazy in that mask and my heavy winter coat.

I pulled off my most successful disguise one time when I met Nick at the Detroit airport to bring him to Toledo. I took my disguise along and changed in the airport's ladies' room. I put on a shoulder-length black wig, long sparkly earrings, and lots of eye makeup. I tucked my jeans into high-heeled boots and put on a bright green rebozo from Venezuela, which is a large, heavy, wool shawl, and walked out to the area where Nick would arrive. Amazingly, none of the women in the restroom asked why I was putting on this costume! In today's world someone would have called the security guards. While waiting for Nick, I stationed myself near a large bank of pay phones—(remember those?)—from which I could see him but he couldn't see me. When he arrived he looked around and seemed puzzled that I wasn't there. He started walking down the long corridor. I waited until he was about ten feet in front of me, and then I started after him. I finally caught up with him, and when I was alongside of him, I suddenly reached out and grabbed his arm. He reacted with an *"Ahhhhh!"* and a horrified look at the creature he was beholding. He was so startled that he dropped his ever-present briefcase!

Only when I said, "Nick, don't you like my hair?" did he realize who it was. We both started laughing so hard that everyone else walking past was laughing too, especially when I took off my wig! Can you imagine this happening in airports today? I would be arrested and spirited away for questioning. It's sad that so much innocent fun has been taken from us because of what the world has become.

ALASKAN ADVENTURE

"*Ay caramba!*" exclaimed the naturalist from Mexico as the humpback whales surfaced in what is called "bubble-net feeding." We were on a small seventy-passenger boat in Alaska, experiencing some of the most marvelous of nature's creatures: whales—humpbacks, orcas, and minkes—and dolphins, porpoises, and seals. Puffins, albatross, Jaegers, and guillemots were among the feathered creatures.

One of the most exciting experiences was our encounter with the humpback whales, who came so close to our boat that we could look down into their blow holes. I stood for hours watching these leviathans breach, slap their great tails, and come in close to our boat to give us the eye. Our ship had two naturalists on board, one of whom was from Mexico and whose expertise was "scat." As we hiked in Glacier National Park, he identified the various scat, especially that of bears, and told us to shout, "Yo, bear!" and clap our hands loudly when we were near bear scat.

Back on board our small ship, we were fortunate enough to see the bubble-net feeding, which none of the passengers nor the two naturalists had ever seen. This is a team effort for humpback whales to catch and eat herring and other small fish. In this case, the team consisted of ten or more whales. There seemed to be a captain calling the plays, which involved all swimming around and around in a circle, under water, of course, causing the herring to be trapped in the middle and to rise to the surface. When an enormous ball of fish was formed, the whale captain would give the signal, and the whole team would rise to the surface with their gigantic mouths open, taking in all the fish. This maneuver was repeated about every eight minutes. Each time those gaping mouths appeared, our Mexican scat expert excitedly yelled, "Ay caramba!" It was a wonder to behold, one I shall never forget.

Our country is blessed to have Alaska belong to us, thanks to William Seward, who purchased it from Russia in 1867. He knew that Seward's Folly, as that purchase was called, would be a wise investment and valuable asset to the United States of America. I only hope the amazing wildlife of Alaska will continue to be appreciated and protected so that future generations will shout, "Ay caramba!" at its wonders.

AN EMOTIONAL JOURNEY

To tour the beaches and towns of Normandy is to take an emotional journey. In this peaceful, beautiful, scenic region of France, it is difficult to imagine the fierce battles and slaughter that took place there in 1944. We visited various museums pertaining to that year and were astonished at some of the primitive instruments of war, such as the gliders, those flimsy contraptions that were easy targets for the Germans. It is a wonder that any Americans survived.

A visit to Point du Hoc makes it clear that the mission here was an impossible one to undertake. American rangers scaled steep cliffs, only to be met by German machine guns in bunkers pointed directly at them, which mowed them down immediately. Yet, miraculously, some survived and took that position from the enemy.

Visiting the German cemetery was also enormously sobering. Such young men died in the belief that it was for their country—so they needed to believe! The tragedy of war overwhelms.

Nothing prepared me for my first view of the American Cemetery, which is located on a bluff above what we now call Omaha beach. It was so named by the Allies under the command of General Dwight D. Eisenhower in the 1944 Normandy landings. To come into the entrance of the cemetery and be greeted by row after row of white crosses as far as the eye could see, seemingly into infinity, was an overwhelmingly emotional experience. Walking among the rows of crosses and reading the names that indicated the ethnic melting pot of our nation, seeing the Star of David on so many of the crosses, made me feel proud of my country but tremendously sad for all those lost lives. The cemetery felt like a sacred place, and it appeared that the other visitors shared that feeling, for no one spoke above a whisper, and many tears were shed.

As my husband and I concluded our visit and were just nearing the exit, a young French couple approached us. They seemed to be between twenty-five and thirty years old. The young man asked in French if we were Americans. When I answered *oui*, he asked me, "*Que ce que c'est ca?*" (What is that?), pointing to a plaque on the ground which we hadn't yet noticed. The plaque had five gold stars on it. The inscription was in English and read, "In memory of General Dwight D. Eisenhower and the forces under his command, this sealed capsule containing news reports of the June 6, 1944 Normandy landings is placed here by the newsmen who were there. June 6, 1969. To be opened June 6, 2044."

I explained that it was a time capsule and translated it into French as best I could. When I finished, the two young people had tears in their eyes. The young man looked at us, took our hands, and said, "*Merci—merci aux Americains.*" With that I burst into tears. It was the first time I had ever heard a young French person express such gratitude for our country's efforts during WWII. It was a moment I shall never forget.

MEETING NEFERTITI

Several years ago, after a bike trip in the Czech Republic, we met our Swiss friends, Hans and Lislott, in Berlin. They were in Germany because of Hans's business, and they had a car. Knowing Berlin very well, they were wonderful guides, taking us everywhere we wanted to go, including the fabulous Pergamon Museum with the astounding Ishtar Gate and Processional Way from the inner city of Babylon. This amazing antiquity was built under King Nebuchadnezzar, and the beauty and splendor of it took my breath away. The Pergamon also houses ancient Greek and Roman architecture that is splendid and awesome.

Hans wanted to show us the (then) new railway station which his electrical company had helped to construct. What a construction it is, with three levels of glass and steel, and apparently totally efficient.

We also visited the new Jewish Museum designed by Daniel Libeskind, which had opened one day before 9/11. I particularly wanted to see it because my daughter, Constance Hauman, had sung in the concert to mark the opening of that hauntingly beautiful building.

The other must-see on my list was the famous bust of Queen Nefertiti, the reputedly exquisitely beautiful wife of Pharoah Akhenaten. My guidebook, which was current, said she was in the Charlottenburg Palace museum, just outside of Berlin proper.

Our friends graciously agreed to drive us there. I remember we had difficulty finding a legal parking place and had to walk quite a distance to reach the entrance of the museum. Just before we paid the entrance fee, I asked in which wing of the museum we would find Nefertiti. We were shocked to learn that she had been moved several weeks before to the Altes Museum—which is next to the Pergamon, from where we had just driven! I was not only shocked, I was furious! How were we going to see Nefertiti? Hans and Lislott had to leave us at four thirty that afternoon in order to get their flight back to Zurich, and we were leaving for the United States the next morning. It was already past three thirty, and we knew the Altes Museum closed at 5:00 p.m., according to my guidebook.

Hans decided he would try to get us there before closing time. He sped back to the city, all of us quite tense at his speed, and we arrived at the big square in front of the museum at exactly four thirty. We bade hasty adieus, jumped out of the car, and hurried as fast as we could go, climbing what seemed like hundreds of stairs to the entrance of the museum. We arrived at the top at four forty, only to be told by a guard that visitors were not allowed in after four thirty! The guidebook didn't mention that!

I burst into tears, explained that we had traveled to Charlottenburg only to be disappointed, showed him my guidebook, and begged him to let us in just to see Nefertiti, nothing else. I told him that it was our one and only chance ever to see her. The guard weakened and let us in, admonishing us not to go anywhere else in the museum and telling us we had to be back at one minute before five. We ran down the long corridor to where Nefertiti was, and it was worth all the sore muscles that came after. What an amazing Queen! I had seen many photos of her but was not prepared for the stunning beauty of this 3,300-year-old woman, who seemed to look straight at us, her beautiful lips starting to smile at us, as if to say, "You see, I am all I have been reputed to be." Her exquisite cheekbones, her graceful neck, the shape of her lovely face, and her perfect brow, made her seem alive, not a painted, stucco-coated limestone sculpture. We devoured her with our eyes and senses, and suddenly it was time to run again. We made it back just as the guard was rattling his keys to the corridor. I breathlessly thanked him profusely and told him I hoped that he knew how fortunate he was to visit that gorgeous woman every day. I think he thought I was a looney, I was so much under her spell.

This time, as we slowly descended the steps to the square, I pondered the beautiful art we had experienced in those few days, much of it made thousands of years ago. How important it is to preserve those works that show what humans can create when we are at our creative best! By the way, if you go to Berlin with the intention of meeting Nefertiti, do check as to her whereabouts. A recent online search revealed her to be housed now in the Neues Museum! I do hope she's enjoying her travels!

SURPRISE AT THE SCHLOSS

Back in the early 1980s, my older daughter spent two months of a summer studying in Graz, Austria, as part of the AIMS Opera program. (This was a well-known program founded by two professional singers from Texas.) Toward the end of her stay, her father and I journeyed to Austria to travel with her. We rented a car and explored the area from Graz, to Linz, to Salzburg and then made our way to Vienna, from where we would fly home. I had planned our trip, and one of the sights I wanted us to visit was a small palace–exactly where I've since forgotten—reputed to have one of the best collections of antiques, especially furniture, in Austria. With my trusty Michelin map and guide, we came to the village where the *Schloss*, or palace, was located. We followed the Schloss signs and the parking signs, but they took us to a *Tiergarten* (zoo). Nearby were some men working on the road, and with my daughter's newly acquired German, we asked for and were given directions to the Schloss. But the roads kept bringing us back to the Tiergarten. We were becoming very frustrated. I had read that the Schloss closed at four, and time was running out. After a few more attempts to reach the Schloss but finding ourselves back at the zoo each time, we parked the car and trudged, grudgingly, along a rough path that pointed to the Schloss. When we finally arrived in the courtyard, it was 4:00 p.m., and there was no one around.

By this time I was really aggravated, and my husband and daughter were not happy campers either. I noticed a door off the courtyard that looked like it might belong to a caretaker, so I knocked. Soon a plump, pretty, blonde, blue-eyed woman in an Austrian (what else?) dirndl opened the door. I asked if she spoke English, and she answered, "Yes—may I help you?" I told her, in my aggravated tone of voice, the whole saga of our trying to find the Schloss and being repeatedly led to the zoo. I explained that we were so disappointed because we would never be in this area again so wouldn't be able to see what we had made the journey to see! She shook her head in understanding, turned, and called, "Heinz, please come."

A stout, ruddy-faced man in his midforties appeared, dressed in what I assumed were his caretaker's clothes: a dark-blue pair of pants and a white, short-sleeved, collared shirt. I told our whole story again and added that we were particularly interested in what we had read was an outstanding collection of rare antique furniture. He instructed us, "Please wait one moment, and I will give you a tour." We were totally surprised. He returned shortly, with an enormous ring of keys, and asked us to follow him. He led us to a sort of back entrance to the Schloss, leading us then into the Hallway of Ancestors. There on the wall of the long hall hung portraits of men dating from four hundred years ago to the present. All of them resembled Heinz—and the last portrait was of Heinz himself! I was totally stunned.

I asked, "Is this your Schloss?"

"Yes," he said. "It has been in my family for many years."

"And do you live here?" I asked.

"My wife, Anna, whom you met earlier, and I live in the former caretaker's quarters, and we only entertain now and then here in the Schloss." He went on to explain about the exorbitant taxes they must pay and the huge expense for upkeep, which was why they opened the Schloss for paying tourists, thus getting tax breaks. I asked about the zoo, which we never did see, and learned that it had always been part of the grounds. He continued to maintain it at great expense.

He toured us through the lovely public and some of the private rooms of the Schloss, explaining details of the furniture, which continued to attract tourists like us. He was so gracious and kind, and he seemed pleased that we were truly interested. When our tour was over, he had not mentioned charging us a fee, and when I asked about it, he said, "Oh, no, no, no. It was my pleasure, and you went to such trouble to find us." Nick asked if we couldn't make a donation toward the upkeep, and Heinz agreed to that. As we were starting to leave, Anna came out of her kitchen, wiped her hands on her apron, and shook our hands goodbye, thanking us for coming! We were treated like guests. Needless to say, my husband and daughter and I were thrilled with this unexpected treat and happy we'd persevered in search of this treasure.

THE PARIS WEDDING

In 1990 my older daughter was married in Paris. She and her husband-to-be had first met in that uniquely enchanting city, and they'd decided that is where the civic wedding would be. It was to take place in the *mairie* of the 3rd arrondissement, with the mairie—or mayor—of the mairie officiating. My husband and I traveled to Paris for the important event. Although I had lived in Paris years before, I had never attended a wedding there, much less a civic wedding, in what I presumed would be a courtroom. I was feeling sad that my daughter's wedding would be so plain.

Along with my husband and me, the wedding party included my daughter's roommate from college and her husband, and friends from the opera world who happened to be in Paris. We were all Americans. We gathered at the appointed hour, my daughter stylish and lovely in a short white suit and a very large white hat. Her friends had given her a huge bouquet of white flowers to hold. The groom looked dashing and handsome.

We entered the courtroom and I was greatly surprised to see how beautiful it was, like a room in a small, ornate palace. But the bigger surprise was the mayor, an attractive, smiling man of about my age. In French he welcomed us all, and then he told us that he felt privileged to be conducting the wedding of two young Americans. He spoke of being a young boy and standing with his parents near this same building when the Americans came to liberate Paris. Seeing the American soldiers parading by, waving, smiling, and being cheered by his people, was a thrill he had never forgotten. He thanked us for giving him this opportunity to do something for us. By then we were all weeping, so moved by this unexpected outpouring of love for us Americans. Such a beautiful and memorable wedding it turned out to be!

KENYA

In the year 2000, my husband, Nick, and I traveled to Kenya. The country was recovering from an almost biblical seven-year drought. The watering holes for the wildlife were dangerously diminished. Lake Nakuru, in the Rift Valley, known for the thousands of flamingos that gathered to eat the lake's algae, had shrunk from ten square miles to three. Sweetwaters, the tented luxury camp made famous by the actor William Holden, had not one blade of green grass. The Masai were known to be bringing their livestock into Nairobi in the middle of the night, to the city parks, to eat the watered, manicured grass. Great numbers of police were called in to try and thwart that activity. It was shocking to see the results of such a prolonged, devastating drought.

Even more shocking were the sights we saw from our ten-person bus as we bumped along on what were called roads but were just potholes strung together by dirt and gravel. In the small villages, which were mostly buildings and huts of corrugated roofing, the men sat next to the road, doing nothing. The only work was being done by women. More substantial houses were surrounded by high stucco block walls with jagged pieces of glass on top and barbed wire above that. In the fields between the villages were hundreds and hundreds of discarded plastic bags, making them look like fields of cotton. There were no receptacles for refuse or garbage anywhere. Our local guide explained that the government ignored any appeal for such containers. The contrast between the wonderful tented camps where we stayed and the real Kenyan world was mindboggling; it made me feel guilty for enjoying such luxury.

Our group, which was sponsored by the Toledo Zoo, had some very special experiences, one of which was a visit to a school. The school served many of the villages but was out in the middle of nowhere. Our guide told us that the children and their parents had to walk miles every day to get to this school. When the parents couldn't accompany a child, that child would miss that day, or maybe a week or more. Many times the older children couldn't attend because they had to help their parents in whatever work was going on.

The school itself consisted of loosely nailed together boards, with cracks you could see through. The classrooms were three-sided, open to the elements. The rooms were strung together in a sort of semicircle. The children all wore uniforms, most of them previously well worn by former students. None of the children wore shoes. There were no blackboards or chalk, just writing paper tacked onto the flimsy walls, with vocabulary, math, and pictures; all were handwritten or drawn. The teachers, who spoke English, were energetic, smiling, and so grateful for the pencils, pens, notebooks, books, and other school supplies which we'd brought to give them; we had been advised in advance that we could do so.

The children were all eager to learn, with bright, excited eyes. We observed some of their lessons. They were respectful and well mannered. At one point a teacher who said she was also the music teacher announced that they would like to sing for us. She escorted the entire population of schoolchildren into the dirt yard, and they sang some songs for us in their language. Then the teacher asked us to sing for them. Our group chose me to lead the singing. We agreed that we all knew "You Are My Sunshine," and we sang it wholeheartedly. The children loved it. They gathered around us, and I taught them to sing it too. After the song fest, the children wanted to touch my hair, I supposed because of the color. One little girl noticed I had on two rings. Both of them were gold but very plain. She asked if I would give her one of the rings. I explained to her that I couldn't do that, because they had been given to me by my family. She then said, "But you have two rings, and I don't have any." If we had not been discouraged from giving such personal items to the children, I would have happily given her one.

Many of the children spoke with other members of our group, proudly speaking the English phrases they had learned. Many of them said, "Please take me home with you." There wasn't a person in our group who left that school unmoved.

If only every young person in this country could have a similar experience! It would help them to understand how privileged they are to have schools to attend, books to study, and buses to transport them! How can we make them see?

Forces of Nature

SONJA AND I

While watching the current Winter Olympic Games, especially the figure skating, I'm taken back to my childhood and my fascination with the first Olympic figure skater, Sonja Henie. I saw her in that iconic movie "Sun Valley Serenade" and was an immediate fan. The girls' restroom in our elementary school was rather long, with a very smooth tile floor, and as often as I could get away with it, I would ask to be excused. Once in the restroom, I would pretend to be Sonja, gliding on the smooth tile floor and imagining I was ice skating. Because I had grown up in the South, ice skating and all winter sports were out of my experience, to be seen only in movies and newsreels. The idea of ever skating or skiing was just an impossible dream, since there were no ice rinks and no snow. Sonja remained only a celluloid idol until I was in my twelfth year. That was when my parents took me to St. Louis, Missouri, to the Ice Capades, where I saw Sonja in person. As the show began, the spotlights made a tight circle, and suddenly there she was, a petite, lovely blonde in a glittering white tutu, a tiara in her hair—a real ballerina on ice! She ran on the tips of her skates, like a little doll, and then skated so fast—twirling, smiling, doing arabesques, tour jetes, leaps, and that amazing spin that resembled film being shown at an incredible speed. I could scarcely breathe! My young heart almost burst with joy while I watched her perform. I will never forget that thrilling evening of seeing my idol skate and dance so beautifully. I wonder if today's skaters remember what they owe to that petite pioneer of the ice.

LEARNING TO SKI

My first snow skiing experience took place in Switzerland, when I was twenty years old. It really didn't count as skiing, because all I did was stand up and fall down, with very little movement in between.

My second serious attempt at skiing was twenty-three years later, in Snowmass, Colorado. By then I was married with two daughters. Inspired by my sister and her family, who had all learned to ski, our family decided to follow in their steps and take a ski trip to their favorite Colorado ski area. We were excited to be doing something new to all of us. Since we didn't own any ski clothes, we went to the local ski shop, where we outfitted ourselves in clothing appropriate for the sport. We looked like seasoned skiers!

After arriving in Snowmass and getting settled in our rented condo, the next step was to rent skis, poles, and boots for our big adventure. I was surprised at the difficulty of trudging through the snow in the heavy boots while carrying skis. I began to have doubts about skiing being fun.

Now came the crucial part—taking a ski lesson. My husband and I took a lesson together, during which the instructor told my husband that he had guts but no style; he told me that I had style but no guts. I thought I had concealed my terror from him. That lesson took place on the "bunny hill," which was a mountain to me as I stood at the top, knowing I had to descend on two unwieldy slats of plastic. We were taught to make small turns and to snowplow. At the end of the lesson we were told to go down the hill on our own. Somehow I managed to pick up unwanted speed, and I realized that even with snowplowing I didn't know how to stop! It seemed to me I was flying down that hill, at the bottom of which was a small ticket booth and a bench on which a woman was sitting. I was headed straight for that bench. I began to yell my warning: "I can't stop! I can't stop!" but unfortunately the woman didn't move. As I crashed into the bench, she recoiled and shouted, "Jesus Christ!"

I lay there sprawled in a heap, saying, "I'm so sorry, so sorry!" She stood, and instead of helping me untangle myself or asking if I were hurt, she marched off in a huff.

After struggling to free myself from my skis so that I could trudge away from the disaster, I realized I had no style as well as no guts. I determined I would change that. At my next lesson the first thing I learned was how to stop the proper way.

Later in that "fun" ski week, I was riding a chair lift with a young woman, and as we rode, I remarked on the seemingly fearless children skiing down the mountain without poles. I expressed my regret at not learning to ski at a young age rather than forty-three. My lift mate then said she thought I looked much younger than that. Of course I was flattered, but later in our conversation she told me that she was legally blind! The balloon of an ego boost, which by then I sorely needed, was cruelly burst.

One might wonder why, after such disastrous beginnings, I continued to ski. I eventually did become a competent skier of intermediate (or "blue") slopes, and even ventured occasionally, but not happily, to the "black" slopes. My daughters loved our ski trips, and so I persevered, even taking ski trips with my second husband and his family.

My last ski trip ended with a bang, literally. I was skiing with Nick, my younger daughter, and my younger sister and her family in Park City, Utah. On this particular day, I stayed on a blue run while the others took a black run. We agreed to meet at the bottom and take one last run together, on blue, of course. I was skiing along, confidently enjoying my skiing ability, when I was hit by an out-of-control snowboarder. I flew up in the air and then fell in a tangle of skis, poles, arms, and legs—some mine and some the snowboarder's. He was saying, "Oh my God, are you okay?" while I was screaming at him repeatedly, "What the hell were you doing?" A ski patroller appeared, berated the snow boarder, helped me up, and checked to see if I had any major injuries, which miraculously I did not. The patroller steadied me on my skis, and I slowly went the rest of the way down with him beside me, until he was certain I could make it.

When I reached our meeting place, my family greeted me not with concern but with annoyance. "Where have you been? We've been waiting and waiting for you. It's about time you showed up." I burst into tears and told about my near-death experience, but no one was sympathetic. "Hurry, or we'll miss the chance to take one last run." No one seemed to care that I had almost been killed!

I never forgot the sound of that snow board behind me or the feeling of being tossed up into the air. That was my final ski adventure. Although I had many pleasant ski trips and experiences between the first and the last, I confess that of all the sports I've had to give up I miss skiing the least.

MY ANGEL

Where did she go? Was she a skier or a ski angel? This is what I've pondered since that day many years ago when I was a beginning skier on the slopes of Snowmass, Colorado.

We enrolled in the ski school, each of us in a different group, and I began to learn how to keep my skis parallel, to traverse down the mountain, to turn, and to snow plow. The instructor said that I had style but no guts!

On the fourth day of ski school, the instructor led my class from the beginner to the intermediate runs. I was feeling rather "gutsy," and by afternoon I became impatient with what I considered the lack of progress from the rest of the class, particularly one woman who constantly asked questions and challenged the instructor. Toward the end of the afternoon, I was eager to return to the condo and join my family. I convinced the instructor, who at that point was becoming exasperated, that I could find my way down, and I left the group.

About thirty minutes later, I found myself not where I expected to be, but on top of what seemed to me the steepest slope I had ever seen. The late afternoon sun was casting long shadows, and I wanted to go home. My confidence had evaporated. I had no guts. I stared down the mountain and knew I couldn't negotiate it. I sat down on my skis and started to cry. I was never going to see my family again.

My frozen body would be discovered by the ski patrol. I continued to sob.

Suddenly, from out of nowhere, a woman was standing beside me. I had not heard her arrive. Dressed in ski clothes, she was on skis and holding ski poles.

"What is the problem?" she asked.

"I can't ski down this mountain. I don't know how. I'm afraid."

Shaking her finger at me, she said, "Now listen here. You are a grown woman. You stop that crying, get up on your skis, and follow me."

"No, I can't. I won't," I sobbed.

"Oh yes, you can and will," she ordered.

She wouldn't leave until I obeyed her. I followed her closely down the scary slope, my eyes riveted to her back. When we finally reached the bottom and I lifted my head to thank her, she vanished! There wasn't a trace of her, not even tracks from her skis—only a very large white dog that trotted across my path at the end of the ski run.

I clomped my way back to the condo, still in my boots and carrying my skis, now sobbing from relief. My family rushed out to see what was wrong. Between sobs I explained all that happened. They thought I was just exhausted and slightly hysterical. But I was and am certain that I had experienced an encounter with an angel—a skiing angel at that!

BIKING DELIGHTS

Some of the great pleasures Nick and I have shared have been our bicycle trips. We have biked in Italy in Tuscany and the Veneto, in France in the Dordogne Valley and in the Vaucluse area of Provence, in the Czech Republic, the Gulf Islands, Vermont, Croatia, Portugal, and Ireland. Each trip provided wonderful sights and experiences. We participated in a cooking class in Tuscany, visited a walnut-oil press and famous cave drawings in the Dordogne, and sailed on a catamaran in the Gulf Islands. We visited Calvin Coolidge's birthplace in Vermont and took ferryboats from island to island in Croatia, along the Dalmatian coast. We visited a small pottery factory in Portugal, where we also rode through cork forests. In the Czech Republic we visited castles and tasted the original Budweiser Beer. We explored the architecture of Palladio in the Veneto and learned step dancing and how to drink Guinness in Ireland. On each trip we met new and interesting people in our bike group, shared fabulous picnics, stayed in chateaux, paradors, monasteries, and quaint hotels, had private tours of museums and palaces, and of course, sampled delicious cuisine and wines.

The very best omelet I ever tasted was in the Dordogne, near Les Eyzies. Nick and I had stopped at a small restaurant where one could lunch en plein air. We were studying the menu, when the charming waitress whispered to us that her mother had just brought in cepes, the delicious mushrooms so coveted in France. She recommended we have an omelet with cepes. I asked why it was such a secret, and she explained, whispering still, that one never admitted to having found cepes, for fear of giving away one's secret finding place. Continuing, she explained that this was the reason one saw people carrying baskets with pine branches or other kinds of leafy camouflage on top; they were trying to hide their find of the precious fungi. We had wondered about that, because we had indeed seen several people with baskets of pine and other branches as we'd biked along the wooded country roads. No wonder the cepes were so treasured—it was a memorable omelet!

Our bike trips were not without challenges. It was not just what seemed to us to be mountainous terrain—and by the way, we quickly learned that when it says "gently rolling hills" in the biking trip catalogues, that is code for extremely steep and difficult hills!— but there were other challenges as well. For example, we had to learn how to use outdoor facilities such as bushes, stone walls, and ditches, and I had to learn how to do that and keep my shoes and socks dry! We miraculously had only one flat tire in all those trips, and once my bike locked as I was climbing a hill. I fell off but managed to roll into a ditch and wasn't hurt—only my pride suffered.

One time in France, I thought I had lost Nick forever. Each day the group leader and guide provided us with explicit typed directions for the routes we were to follow from the time we set off in the morning until we arrived at our designation in the late afternoon. On this particular day, I was riding behind Nick, as I usually did, and none of the rest of our group was with us. Most had already finished the route and had made a turn, which Nick missed. I saw that he had missed it and was yelling loudly to him, but he couldn't hear me because we were then on a major, heavily trafficked road heading into a large town. He was so far ahead of me that I couldn't catch up to him, and of course he didn't look back to see whether I was following him. Finally I stopped and yelled, "My darling Nick, have a nice life!" I fully expected never to see him again, knowing he didn't speak French and that, being a man, he would not ask for directions! While I was wondering what to do—we didn't have cell phones then—our guide fortunately came along in the "sag wagon" or van. I waved her down and explained the situation. By then, Nick was nowhere to be seen. The guide assured me she would find him, so I pedaled on to our hotel. An hour passed, and still no Nick. Finally the guide returned with him. He had ultimately recognized his error but been unable to find anywhere to turn around safely because of the heavy traffic, so he'd just had to keep riding.

From then on he paid closer attention to the directions, and once in a while he even looked back to see whether I was still behind him!

CHICKS AND DUCKS, DOGS
AND BIRDS, OH MY!

In my childhood back in the 1940s, Easter Sunday was very special. Not only did we dress up in our very best to attend church, we all wore corsages of roses, or carnations, or other sweet-smelling flowers. My mother sometimes had an orchid corsage. The really special treat was what the Easter Bunny brought us: little fluffy, dyed live chicks. We would have multi colors of blue, pink, or green—different colors each year. These chicks never lived very long, probably poisoned by having been dyed. One year, instead of chicks we received three darling little yellow ducklings. They followed my sisters and me as if we were their parents. It didn't take long before they started growing. We removed them from their little box in our house to a much larger box on our back screened-in porch. From time to time we let them out to roam in the backyard, happily eating grass and bugs. They grew into beautiful white ducks. When we wanted them to come to us we would call, "Here Diddle, Diddle, Diddle," and they would come running and quacking to us. They seemed to love us, as we loved them.

The three ducks eventually became so large that my mother decided we should take them to the city park, where there was a small lake with lots of other ducks. It was a sad day when we called, "Here Diddle, Diddle, Diddle," put them in a cage, put it in the back of our station wagon, and took them to the park. We released them and led them to the lake. At first they were reluctant to get into it. They had never been in such a large body of water. Their only experience had been a round metal tub of water in our backyard. They finally ventured in and swam toward the other ducks. We waved good-bye, and my mother drove us home.

The next day we went back to see our ducks. We called, "Here Diddle, Diddle, Diddle," and our three, who were swimming together, swam to us, got out of the pond, and waddled to see us. We repeated these visits for several days. As time passed, it took longer for our ducks to respond to us, and one day, even though we could see them and recognize them, they ignored our pleading calls. Oh, how sad we were! How could they forget us? We were broke hearted. My mother tried to soothe us by explaining that nature was following its course, that our ducks were adults now and had to find their own way and have their own families. She softened the blow by saying that the love we had given them would pass on to their babies. Years later her words still resonate—because isn't that what we all hope for?

Several years later my little sister received more ducklings for Easter. Only one of them survived to adulthood. This duck was a real pet, more like a dog than a duck. One day the duck was attacked by a neighbor's dog, and the poor duck was severely injured. Mother, who always wanted to be a nurse or a doctor, like her country-doctor father, took it upon herself to nurse that duck back to health. She cleaned its wounds, wrapped them, and medicated them daily. The duck was a sight to see, waddling around like a motorized bandage. Sadly, in spite of Mother's ministering, the duck died. It was a huge disappointment to her that she hadn't been able to keep it alive. Mother didn't allow herself to be sentimental about ducks or birds or other pets, but she gave her unconditional love to her family.

We almost always had a dog. One of our favorites was a beautiful Dalmatian named Kate; she was the gentlest of dogs. When my baby sister, Janet, was a toddler, Kate would never leave her side. She would walk protectively beside her with every step Janet took. Kate had puppies, and we kept the pick of the litter, a handsome male we named Dan because his markings made him look very dapper. He grew to be larger than his mother and was a born troublemaker. In our neighborhood the milkman delivered the milk in cartons every morning. His customers started complaining that when they went to bring in their milk, the cartons would be split open and the milk all over their back doorsteps. It was a great mystery, until one morning the culprit was caught in the act. It was our Dan! After that we kept him indoors until later in the morning, after the milk had been delivered and collected. But his troublemaking wasn't over.

One day a neighbor lady was giving an afternoon tea, as many ladies did back then. She had made exquisite little tea sandwiches and cookies and had put them on her back screened-in porch the morning of the tea. She looked out to check on them, and to her horror, there was Dan! He had managed to open the screen door and was devouring all the little treats with great gusto. Our neighbor was livid! She threatened to have the police come and shoot our miscreant pet. She had forgiven him drinking her milk, but this was too much! Mother decided it was time to find a farm home for Dan, which she did, and that was the last we saw of him. Mother assured us that Dan would be well loved and cared for, that he would have plenty of room to run and roam, and that he wouldn't get into so much trouble.

We often had a bird—a parakeet or a canary. One time we had a cat that ate our canary. I remember we returned home in the evening and were greeted by the cat with a feather still hanging on his mouth. Inside, we saw the birdcage overturned and all its contents on the floor, but no sign of the bird. Later the cat disappeared. We never had another cat.

We named all our canaries Biddie. Our very last Biddie developed a strange disease. His toenails grew and grew—like an avian Howard Hughes—and Mother tried to trim them. This didn't work out very well. Eventually Biddie became so ill that he would fall off his perch and lie on his back, struggling to breathe. Mother would reach into his cage, pick him up, say encouraging words, and put him on his perch, only to have him fall off again. One day when I was visiting from far-off Ohio, Biddie fell off his perch, obviously suffering, and I said, "Mother, you really need to do something about Biddie."

She replied, "You think so, do you?"

"Yes," I said. "He's pitiful and suffering."

A few minutes later, Mother took Biddie's cage to the kitchen, I assumed to clean it. Soon she returned, saying, "Well, Biddie's gone."

I said: "What do you mean, he's gone? What did you do?"

"I just pulled his head off, so he's out of his misery," was the answer.

I was shocked, although I shouldn't have been. After all, she had wrung many a chicken's neck in the past—but this was unexpected! I said, "Mother, you didn't!"

"Well, you told me to do something, so I did. You should be glad that Biddie won't suffer anymore," she said. And that was that!

ENCOUNTER WITH A ROYAL (TERN)

Many years ago, in the seventies, while visiting my parents at Point Brittany in St. Petersburg, Florida, I had an encounter with a royal tern. Adjacent to the Point Brittany condos and apartments, there was an east-west island with no houses on it; it was primarily a bird sanctuary. There was a road in preparation for the development which would eventually bring huge houses to that island. Before the houses, there were so many birds there that often in the early morning we had to close the windows to diminish the cacophony of squawking and bird calls announcing the dawn.

One day, while riding my bike on that island, I came upon a large flock of royal terns and stopped to observe. All of them were on the ground, moving about, some making short flights and returning, except one that wasn't moving at all. It occasionally would attempt a movement but would be unsuccessful. Soon the flock took flight— except for that one. I was convinced it was hurt. I parked my bike and moved close to it. Again it tried to move but could not. I was quite distressed. I didn't want to leave it there alone and hurt, but I had no choice. I remembered reading about the Suncoast Seabird Sanctuary, located at Indian Shores, north of St. Petersburg beach, so as I pedaled back to my parents' apartment, I decided to call and see what they could do for my royal tern.

The man with whom I spoke asked where exactly this bird was, what was he doing, and whether I would go back there and wait for him to arrive. I pedaled back, hoping the bird was still alive, and he was. I waited by him for about thirty minutes until a small red truck appeared. A tall, pleasant-looking man got out, took a large cage out of the back of the truck, and walked over to where I was patiently standing guard. He introduced himself as being from the Suncoast Seabird Sanctuary, which eased my mind, because there was no identification on the truck. I asked what he thought was wrong, and he said it could be that the bird had swallowed some plastic, such as a piece of straw or some other item discarded by a careless human. He then walked stealthily up to the bird, and with a movement so quick it startled me, he grabbed the bird by the feet. Then he put it in the cage. He said he would take it to the sanctuary's hospital, where they would make a diagnosis and go from there. I asked if I could call to find out the result, and he gave me a number and an ID number for the bird. Then he said that I was welcome to come visit the bird while it was hospitalized. He got in the truck and drove off, my royal tern caged in the rear.

The next day I phoned to learn the diagnosis. It seems my royal tern was a male, and as it was explained to me, sometimes during mating season (which it then was) a male would simply exhaust himself mating until he could no longer move. Apparently that is what my tern had done! He would remain in the hospital for a few days in order to fully recover.

The next day, my parents and I drove up to Indian Shores to visit my sexually overactive tern. It was our first of several visits to that amazing place. My first reaction was one of anger—to see birds maimed for life because of humans and their carelessness with their boats, fishing equipment, and detritus. Then I felt gratitude for this special place, which rehabilitates some of the birds and releases them back to the wild. The others are cared for until they die. Birds born there are released as soon as they are able to be on their own.

We went into the hospital to visit my bird. The hospital was all white, clean, and neat, with the "doctors" in white coats. The smaller birds, like my tern, were in little white cubicles, stacked in several rows. The doctors and volunteers were attentive to their patients. My bird was pointed out to me, and I was told that he was doing well and would be released the next day.

The entire visit was extremely moving and educational. It was sobering to learn that nine out of ten bird injuries are caused directly or indirectly by humans. It is so important that the Suncoast Seabird Sanctuary continues to operate and have visitors, especially young people, to help educate them about the importance of respecting nature's gifts. If you've never been there, I urge you to go.

Today when I bike on that island, now called Bayway Isle, and see all the large houses, I can't help but feel sad that it is no longer a refuge for our seabirds. We've stolen so much habitat from nature's creatures to have it for ourselves. Will we ever stop?

WATCHING BIRDERS WATCH BIRDS

Every May, northwest Ohio is host to hundreds of nature's feathered and winged marvels—birds. They come to the shores of Lake Erie, where they rest for days before continuing their journeys across the lake to points north in Canada. One of their favorite resting spots is at Magee Marsh, about one hour's drive from our home in Toledo. For two weeks, our community and those nearby are inundated with birders from all over the world, eager to add to their lists of warblers and other feathered species.

One year my husband and I drove to Magee Marsh with great anticipation of participating in what is now called the Biggest Week in American Birding. As we entered the area, we were amazed to see a huge tent filled with binoculars, cameras, and tripods of every size and shape for sale—commercialism in all its grandeur. We were directed to the parking area, where there were license plates from almost every one of our fifty states, many on RVs and SUVs with camping equipment attached to them.

We parked our car and went to explore. The first thing we noticed was that our binoculars were miniscule compared to what these serious birders had hanging from their necks and shoulders. We were almost embarrassed to be among them! Many of these birders were dressed as if on an African safari: khaki pants and shirts, with multiple pockets containing notebooks, pens, and other essential birding equipment. In our ordinary shorts and T-shirts, we stuck out like the amateur birdwatchers we were.

A sign told us we could take a tour with a professional birder if we met at a certain time and place. There would be room for only twelve people, so we went immediately to the place to await the appointed time. Soon the pro arrived, a delightful man from Australia who had made studying birds his life's work. He explained the rules: no talking above a whisper and no wandering away from the group. Then we started on the search. He could spot the tiniest of little warblers. He would tell us where it was, and we would all try to focus our "binos" to see what he saw. He would tell us the names—so many different names for birds that looked alike to us!

The birds weren't flying about; they were too tired and were nestled in the bushes and trees resting. We spotted gorgeous little yellow warblers and American redstarts. We came to one area where Baltimore orioles were hanging from the branches of a large bush, looking like orange ornaments on a Christmas tree.

We had walked to the shore of the lake, when our professional said, "Oh my gosh! Here is something I've never before seen!" He told us to look out over the lake, where we could just make out a tiny, dark moving object. It was a lone bird trying to make it to shore from the middle of Lake Erie! Suddenly it plummeted into the water and didn't come up. "Oh no, he's a goner!" we all said. But no—in a minute it rose from the water, struggling to fly and continue. It did so for a few minutes, but then down it went again. "Oh no, this time it won't make it," we cried. But again, out of the lake it rose and flew a few more minutes before crashing again into Lake Erie. By this time our pro, with his gigantic binos, had identified the bird not a waterfowl, as he had first thought, but an ordinary blackbird! This nonswimming bird continued his monumental effort, falling into the water and then rising again like a phoenix to continue. Now we were all cheering it on: "Keep going! You'll make it, you'll make it!" we called to it.

Finally this courageous, persistent, determined bird made it to a tree on the shore. We broke all the rules of being quiet and were yelling and applauding, even shedding tears for this little creature's victory. It was a truly moving experience, one I'll never forget, and it forever changed the way I look at a blackbird!

EXCITEMENT OF THE ECLIPSE

On August 20, 2017, my husband and I made the eight-hour drive to my sister's home in Madisonville, Kentucky, in order to view the total eclipse of the sun on August 21. Madisonville, a small town in Western Kentucky, was one of the towns in the path for the total eclipse. As we made the drive south, it seemed everyone else also was headed in that direction, judging by the traffic we encountered. We arrived at Janet's house in the late afternoon. My other sister had arrived earlier, bringing her granddaughter and her daughter-in-law. It was a real family reunion with me, my husband, and my two sisters and members of their families. My hostess sister had provided the necessary glasses for all of us to watch the eclipse.

Madisonville was named for President James Madison, who had stayed in Madisonville at one point. There is an historic house in which he spent some time. In his honor, T-shirts had been designed with a portrait of Madison wearing eclipse glasses, and my sister had purchased one for each of us to wear on the big day.

My sister's home was located in a neighborhood of houses set on large pieces of property, from which there were unobstructed views of the sky. Her house had a swimming pool on the large side lawn by their house, which was a welcome place for relaxing in the West Kentucky summer heat.

The day of the 21st was beautiful, with not a single cloud in the sky, and 90 degrees, so the pool was our location of choice as we waited for the big moment. All of us donned our swimsuits and enjoyed the cooling balm of the pool. Then, before the eclipse was to begin, we put on our glasses and T-shirts to honor the occasion of a first total eclipse for each of us.

As the eclipse began, one of my sisters said, "When it reaches totality, don't anyone say a word until it's over. Let's watch in silence." We all agreed. The eclipse began shortly after noon, at 12:26. As the shadow of the moon began to pass across the sun, the cicadas started their music, and the birds twittered and flew into the trees. The temperature began to fall into a comfortable 75 degrees—a drop of fifteen degrees in just minutes. There was no wind, not even a slight breeze.

When the eclipse reached totality, we could see the amazing corona, and soon after that the "diamond ring"—such a gorgeous sight. I removed my glasses to look around and see how dark it had become. To my surprise it was not dark as night but more like evening just before darkness comes, because so much light was emanating from the corona. Quickly I put on my glasses again, so as not to miss the remaining totality. As the sun gradually began to reappear, there was a sudden whoosh wind; it was strong but fleeting.

All of us were awestruck by what we had just witnessed. I felt unexpectedly emotional—a combination of awe and humility at our ignorance of the mysteries of our universe, and an overwhelming sense of being such a miniscule part in the whole of it.

Later that afternoon we resumed our swimming and visiting, and that night at dinner we discussed our reactions. We had all shared the same sense of awe and amazement. We had discovered the true meaning of *awe*some.

ARMS AND THE WOMAN

Author Nora Ephron wrote a book called "I Feel Bad About My Neck." She expressed what many women feel as they age. Personally, I don't feel as bad about my neck as I do my arms. I read once that if you want to know what your arms will look like when you are "a certain age," just look at your mother's arms. My arms are now like my aging mother's were, with sagging flesh from the elbow to the armpit. I call these "Lady Bird Johnson" arms. Remember when the camera would show Lady Bird waving to people while wearing short sleeves, and the underneath part of her arm would move in the opposite direction, like a flag flapping in the breeze? That's what my arms do now, in spite of my having done upper-arm exercises for years in an attempt to ward off this curse.

Sometimes my underarms move independently from the rest of my arms. I catch them out of the corner of my eye pulling this dirty little trick. I learned years ago to never use a salt or pepper shaker while wearing a sleeveless blouse, or to wave to someone at a distance without raising my arm totally straight and then waving from the elbow up. If I want to give a small wave to someone nearby, I know to hold my arm tight against my torso and wave from the wrist.

This arm situation has changed what I notice in women. Instead of eyes, mouth, hair, height, weight, or wrinkles, I notice arms. I covet those that are slim and nonwiggly, and I'm grateful mine are not as bad as some.

I go to the dermatologist yearly for a checkup, and he dictates to his nurse that I have "litiginies" here, there, and everywhere on my body. I asked him once why he insists on using a euphemism instead of calling them what they are: age spots, or liver spots, as my mother called them. He just smiled at me kindly and continued recording the "litiginies"—I know what they are, and I don't like them!

I'm glad I continue to age, because that means I'm still alive, but I wish age didn't insult our bodies the way it does. To quote a French philosopher: "*Je lute contre l'outrage de l'age*"—I struggle against the outrage of age!

FAMILY

A HOT TIME

When I married my husband, Nick Dye, in the summer of 1988, I moved to Wausau, Wisconsin to live with him. I had always thought that Wisconsin would be like Michigan—freezing in the winter but lovely and cool in the summer. I moved into the townhouse where Nick had already lived for a year. It was very nice, on two levels. The living room, dining area, kitchen, and master bedroom and bath were on the top level, and it had two other bedrooms and a large family room on the slightly lower-than-ground level. The problem was, there was no air-conditioning. Hardly anyone in Wausau had air-conditioning, because it was seldom needed—until that summer, which proved to be one of the hottest in Wisconsin history!

One day, for some crazy reason, I decided to show Nick my Southern cooking skills. The kitchen was quite small, but I thought I could manage the menu I had planned to surprise him. As the day progressed and became hotter and hotter, I had second thoughts, but since I had purchased all the ingredients, I decided to go ahead with my plan. Late that afternoon I began. I made cornbread, which meant using a hot oven. I fried chicken and eggplant patties. By the time Nick came home, fresh corn on the cob was boiling, as were fresh green beans. I had prepared Dixie relish (tomatoes, cucumbers, and onions in vinegar, sugar, and water), and the chicken and eggplant patties were frying away. Sweat was pouring down my face and body, and when Nick walked into the kitchen, he could barely see me for the steam rising from the stove. He looked tired and bedraggled, with his tie loosened and his jacket dragging. He asked, "What on earth are you cooking?" I named everything enthusiastically.

"Can't you just turn it all off, and let's go to a movie or something?" he said.

"Turn it off? You can't just turn off fried chicken and eggplant patties," I said, huffily. "Once you start it you have to finish, and cornbread can't be cooked just halfway."

"Well," said he, "I don't feel like eating any of that. It's too damn hot!"

"What? After I've gone to all this trouble, you don't want it?"

"No, I don't, not now."

I said, much louder, "How can you say that? I wanted to show you that I can really cook Southern."

"Well, I'm going downstairs where it's cooler. I need my space," said he.

"Your space? I've been slaving away in this tiny kitchen to please you. Let me tell you something, Mr. Dye," I said, shaking my cooking utensil vigorously. "I'll never fry chicken for you again, even if you come crawling, begging for it!"

With that I finished all the cooking, stored some of it, threw some of it away, and went to find my own space.

Our marriage survived that very hot round, but I did not fry chicken for at least ten years after that—and no one came begging for it either!

FRIED CHICKEN

When I was growing up we ate a lot of fried chicken. I remember watching my mother or the maid preparing it. Wearing big aprons, they would soak the chicken in cold water and then take the pieces, dripping wet, and put them in a bowl of flour to coat each piece thoroughly. Then they would put the pieces into a large iron skillet, with plenty of very hot melted Crisco, and fry it to a crisp, golden brown. The sizzling sound of the frying and the smell from the kitchen were tantalizing. I loved eating the "brickle," as we called it, which was the fried crust that fell off the chicken while it cooked. My favorite piece was the "pulley bone," or the piece from the very center of the breast, also called the wish bone. After that delicious piece of chicken had been eaten, two people would pull on that bone until it broke, and whoever got the shortest piece could make a wish. (Sometimes it was the longest piece, depending on who made the rules.)

During the years of WWII, when people had victory gardens and raised rabbits, ducks, chickens, and other fowl for food, my mother raised a few chickens for our consumption. I remember the chicken coop, which was behind our garage, hidden from the neighbors by the wall along the very back part of our yard. The coop was about five feet tall, and I would go out and talk to the chickens as only a child can. At first I didn't realize those were the chickens we had been eating. One day when my mother was going out to the coop and I started to go along, she stopped me and told me to stay inside. I wondered why and decided to spy from behind the curtains in our breakfast room, which faced the backyard. What I saw was my mother and the maid each grabbing a chicken by the neck, one in each hand, and slinging them around and around and around. Then they gave a great pull, and off came the chickens' heads! I recall closing the curtains and opening them, closing and opening—I didn't want to see, and yet I did want to see. The horrible, fascinating thing was that chickens' bodies and wings continued to move, and they flapped around the yard even without their heads!

Finally I closed the curtains and ran upstairs to my room. I couldn't imagine my wonderful mother being able to do such a thing, even though I knew she had grown up on a farm. Somehow, I had never associated fried chicken for dinner with what I had just witnessed.

I never mentioned my spying and in fact watched a similar scene more than once; I was always amazed at the headless bodies flapping away on the ground. In spite of that horror, I continued to relish eating fried chicken, especially for Sunday dinner.

As an adult I also learned to fry chicken, although I purchased my chickens at a market. My own daughters loved my fried chicken, just as I had loved my mother's. As the years went by, Mother complained that chicken just didn't taste as good as in former times. She said it was because chickens no longer had mothers to teach them how to peck for grass, worms, bugs, and other natural foods but were born, raised, and transported in crowded pens with no room to move. To quote her, "Chickens today are just idiot chickens!" The memory of delicious home-fried chicken propels me to fry it once a year, and when I do, I savor the smell, the sound, the brickle, and the pulley bone. I try not to remember those images of my long-ago childhood and just hope that the chicken I'm about to eat was not an idiot, that it had a mother that taught it how to be a natural chicken!

STARRING MY FAMILY

In 1956 my father was a delegate to the Republican Party Convention held in San Francisco, in the Cow Palace. The main purpose of the convention was to nominate Dwight Eisenhower for a second term as President of the United States. Through the help of Senator Thruston Morton of Kentucky, I was appointed a page for the Kentucky delegation, and my younger sister Linda was selected as a "special" page (girls and boys of fourteen or fifteen), so our whole family made the trip to California. My duty as a page was to deliver any messages from members of the Kentucky delegation to other delegates, chairmen, and assorted politicians. This was before cell phones, emails, texting, etc., and the messages were handwritten or just given verbally.

Linda's duties required her and her young colleagues to appear on the large stage carrying or wearing banners announcing a variety of information; they were always ushered in by the newscaster John Chancellor. My mother and my littlest sister, Janet, who was eight, sat in the visitor sections with relatives of senators and delegates. Somehow, people working on the Will Rogers Junior morning TV show learned that an entire family from the exotic-sounding small town of Paducah, Kentucky was attending the convention, and we were asked to be on the show—an invitation my father gladly accepted. The bad news was that we had to be up and dressed for our appearance at 3:00 a.m.! That was extremely difficult, but it was worth the effort. Will Rogers Junior was very gracious. He held Janet on his lap while we met Randolph Churchill, Winston's son, who was appearing as a commentator about the convention. We were asked questions about what we did, what sights we hoped to see, and how we felt about being at the convention. We seemed like the perfect family. Everyone in our hometown was thrilled to see us on national TV. Interestingly, many years later each member of our family remembered what he or she had been wearing. I can still see my yellow-and-white silk full-skirted dress and yellow shrug jacket. I wish I had saved it!

The conventioneers had no trouble renominating Ike, and since there wasn't that much work to be accomplished, there was plenty of entertainment, including Nat King Cole, Irving Berlin, and Jane Powell, to mention a few. I was thrilled to see Jane Powell, because she had been one of my silver-screen idols. I had a close encounter with her in a hallway, and her demeanor didn't disappoint. We also saw many other celebrities, not only movie stars but newsmakers as well. I remember seeing Harold Stassen and being amazed by his huge head—larger than a pumpkin! Richard Nixon was the vice-presidential nominee, and he was actually quite handsome, although he never looked it on TV.

One of the highlights of the week for me was playing a small part in a reunion. Every day a minister or rabbi from a different state would offer an opening prayer. On one occasion, a delegate from another state, passing me and seeing my page's badge, asked me to deliver a message to the minster who had just given the prayer. He thought the minister had been the chaplain of his unit in WWII, whom he hadn't seen since. Upon receiving the message, the minister's eyes widened, his mouth dropped open, and he asked me to take him to that delegate. When they saw one another, they opened their arms and clasped each other in a warm embrace, tears in their eyes, so that I, too, was shedding tears. It was such a joyous reunion, and I was happy to have helped facilitate it.

On the rare occasions that I watch current political party conventions, I marvel at how different they are from that one in 1956. I'm sure there was plenty of silliness that I don't remember, but I remember it as being much more dignified that what I've seen recently. I'm happy to have that memory.

A SURPRISING REVELATION

Christmas Eve with my family was always very special. It meant getting together with my father's two brothers and their wives and children, all of whom lived in our town. Sometimes my other aunt, "your father's only sister," as she always said, would drive with her husband the several hours from where they lived to join us. Occasionally my grandfather and step-grandmother also would come.

It was quite a festive occasion. My mother and my two aunts would each take a turn being hostess once every three years. The table would be set with the best silver, china, and crystal. The dinner would be sumptuous, with country ham, turkey, dressing, sweet potatoes, and all sorts of other dishes. Then would come the amazing desserts: chess pie, pecan pie, boiled custard, ambrosia, and caramel cake, to name but a few selections. Everyone would dress up in party clothes, the men in coats and ties and the women in silks, satins, and sequins. After dinner we would all sing carols. Each home had a piano, and either one of us "kids" or my mother would play while we all sang. We drew names for gift exchange, which provided much merriment, especially because my father's "only sister" never remembered who had given her what, and many times the giver became the recipient of her gift the following year! As the family grew and we "kids" became adults, married, and had children, dinner became a grand buffet, with seating anywhere one could find a place. We still sang carols after dinner, and all of our children would perform. It was wonderful while it lasted. Eventually families went in different directions and couldn't always come home to Paducah from faraway places. Those memories are so dear to me—there was so much love there.

Christmas Day was always shared with my mother's sister and her husband and children. This group wasn't as numerous as my father's clan. Sometimes a family-less couple, longtime friends of my aunt and my mother, would join us. We always had dinner in the afternoon, and it was a lavish repeat of the Christmas Eve event. I often wondered how my mother managed when it was her turn to have both Christmas Eve and Christmas Day dinners. We sometimes sang carols on Christmas Day but not as lustily as on Christmas Eve. Of course this tradition came to an end also, but the love that was shared never did. My immediate family, along with my aunts, uncles, and cousins, were loving and caring. We cherished our relationships not just at Christmastime but every day.

Then, when I was thirty years old, I had a surprising revelation: my perfect family wasn't so perfect! I was spending time in my parents' home with my children while my husband was doing his annual army reserve duty of two weeks. It was then that I learned about my father's and my uncles' other lives.

I was sitting on my mother's front screened-in porch with her and her sister, when suddenly my aunt said, "Yonder he goes!"

"Who goes?" I asked.

"Oh, never mind," was the answer.

"Well, we know where he's going," said my aunt, with great disgust in her voice.

They immediately changed the subject, but after my aunt had left, I pressed my mother to tell me what that had been about. She proceeded to tell me everything.

For years my own dear father, who adored my mother and doted on me and my two sisters, had had a succession of mistresses! The first one had been when I was only one or two years old. My mother had been heartbroken to make this discovery and had wanted to divorce my father, but her father, my grandfather, had convinced her that she and I would have a much better life if she stayed with my father, who had now sworn to be faithful ever after.

As the years went on, there were other mistresses. Once, when my very young daughters were spending time at my parents' home, my father was holding my younger daughter, who was just a baby at the time, when the phone rang. My mother answered. It was one of my aunts, who told my mother that the woman who was my father's current mistress had just died. My mother hung up the phone, turned to my father, and said, "I've just had the most wonderful news. Jane Doe has just died!" My father was so shocked he almost dropped my baby daughter on the floor, but of course he couldn't say anything!

Later Mother told me about the time she decided to catch my father with his latest girlfriend. She called my father's brother, a sweet, sentimental soul who was devoted to his family and to my mother. She told him to come and take her to my father's girlfriend's house, and when he did, they found my father's car in the driveway. My mother climbed up on the hood of his car and looked in the kitchen window, where she saw my father with his arm around this woman, with neither of them fully clothed. She rapped on the window, and on seeing my mother, they ran into another room. My mother then took a baseball bat, which she had brought with her, and with all the power of her five-feet, one-inch petite self, she bashed in the back door, to the horror of my uncle, who kept urging her to leave and go home. She entered the house, where she found my father under a bed with nothing on but his boxer shorts, his shoes and socks, and his hat on his head! My mother mocked him and his girlfriend, and then she and my uncle left. My father was very contrite for months, but he later resumed seeing "that woman."

As for that sweet, sentimental uncle, he too had girlfriends. He met his lady friends after church on Sundays. He would attend church with my aunt and then afterwards say he had a business deal he had to see about. (He, like my father, was an automobile dealer.) When my aunt, not even five feet tall, discovered the truth about his "business," she waited until one night when he was in their bed, and she took his belt and started beating him with it. At any time he could have overpowered her, because he was six feet tall and strapping, but he lay there and let her beat him until her little arm gave out!

Another of my father's brothers would often come to our house, crying, with stories of how his wife abused him, verbally and physically. He was also about six feet tall, and my aunt was a small but determined woman. Their household was so volatile that many time, my cousins would come spend the night at our house in order to escape the turmoil. Once, my aunt, who had many physical problems, found my uncle in the bed with her nurse! I think that was the time she pulled a gun on him and threatened to kill him!

My mother's sister's husband was my father's business partner. This aunt would regularly brag about how *her* husband would never philander. At one point mother learned that this was not so, and when my aunt began bragging about my uncle's faithfulness compared to my father's, mother decided to tell her the truth.

To prove it, one night Mother drove my aunt to my uncle's girlfriend's house. (In my hometown everyone knew everything about everybody.) They looked in the window of the living room (no one drew their curtains), and there sat my uncle, with his arm around this younger woman. His car was parked in front, and he had left it unlocked. My aunt told my mother to go on home, while she got into the back seat of my uncle's car and waited, hunkered down where he couldn't see her. After a while he came out of the house, whistling and happy, got into the car, and started to drive away. Imagine his surprise when my aunt raised herself and made herself known—my uncle almost crashed the car! That was the end of the girlfriend and also my aunt's bragging.

When I first heard these stories I was shocked and saddened, but as time went on, I found them amusingly absurd. My father and my uncles had always been pillars of their community and of their churches, and their philandering never seemed to tarnish their reputations. Amazingly enough, these husbands and wives continued to love each other deeply until their deaths; they never wavered in their devotion to each other and to their families.

So the question remains: What is a "perfect" family? Maybe mine was perfect after all.

A TERRIFYING INTRUSION

From the time I was first married and moved away from my home in Paducah, Kentucky, I telephoned my mother frequently. We had always been close, and I missed being able to talk with her on a daily basis. For years we spoke by telephone at a minimum of once a week, sharing our thoughts, our activities, and as my daughters were growing up, talking about their progress and accomplishments.

When both my parents were in their early seventies, my father suffered a massive stroke, after which he spent many weeks in a rehab center. I telephoned Mother often, knowing that she was alone in her house every night. I usually asked, "How are you? Has Daddy shown any improvement? What have you been doing besides going to see him? Have you been with any of your friends? Are you okay?"

One night when I phoned to ask these questions, I knew by the tone of her voice that something was wrong, even though she said she was okay. "I can tell something is wrong. What is it?"

"Oh, nothing."

"Yes, I know there is something wrong. Tell me what has happened."

"You must promise you won't tell your sisters if I tell you."

"I promise. For heaven's sake, tell me what it is!" And so she began to tell about the horrifying intrusion.

The night before my call she had gone upstairs to get ready for bed and then come downstairs to lock all the doors in the house. This entailed locking the front door and putting the safety chain in place, locking the French doors that led to the glassed-in porch, locking the door that led from the kitchen to the driveway, and finally, going into the family room, opening the door that led into the one-car garage, stepping into the garage, and pushing the button that closed the garage door, which for some reason she always left open until bedtime. She would then step back into the family room, close and lock that door, and go upstairs, feeling secure after performing the locking ritual.

That night, as she stepped into the garage, a man had grabbed her from behind, clamped his hand over her mouth, and said, "Don't scream, and I won't hurt you." He then tied a blindfold over her eyes and led her into the house, commenting on what he saw as he led her from room to room. He didn't seem interested in the silver or any other valuable object, but led her upstairs. She was terrified but made herself appear calm. As they reached the landing at the top of the stairs that led into the master bedroom suite, he commented on the bridal portraits of me and each of my sisters, saying, "Oh yes, she's the one who lives in Lexington, and that one is the youngest, who lives in Madisonville, and there's the oldest, the one who studied in Paris and now lives in Toledo." His voice sounded familiar, and he certainly knew all about us, which frightened Mother even more. Then he said, "I know you keep your jewelry in the bedroom. Where is it?"

"In the back bedroom, in the dresser." He led her into that room and told her to touch a piece of furniture and tell him if that were the dresser.

"Is there a mirror over it?"

"Yes."

"Then this is the one."

The intruder began opening all the drawers and asked, "Where is your gold coin pendant?" This man even knew her jewelry! Mother explained that she had recently taken some of her jewelry to her lock box at the bank, and the pendant was among what she'd taken. He continued going through drawers and boxes, and as she later discovered, took her favorite earrings, her diamond watch, a bracelet, and several other small pieces. Fortunately, she also had taken her rings to her lock box.

After pocketing the jewelry, he moved her into the dressing room, where he demanded that she perform a certain sex act. She heard him unzip his pants. She felt sick.

"First, he said, "Take out your teeth."

"Take out my teeth? I can't take them out."

"You mean they are your own teeth?"

"Of course they're my own teeth. Whose teeth do you think they are?"

The knowledge that her teeth were permanent seemed to change the pervert's mind, because to her great relief, she heard him zip up his pants. He then sat her on her dressing table chair and told her to remain there blindfolded until he had made his departure.

"If you call the police, I'll come back, and this time I'll hurt you. When you hear me leave, wait ten minutes before you remove the blindfold. Remember, I'll know if you have called the police or anyone else."

Mother did as she was told. She had read that it took exactly one minute to recite the Lord's Prayer as one would in church, so she repeated it ten times, and twice more to be on the safe side. Then she took off the blindfold and bravely went downstairs to lock the door to the garage. She went up to bed and relived the entire episode, not falling asleep until the wee hours of the morning.

She told me she thought she knew the identity of the culprit, that she'd recognized the voice of the only male beautician at the beauty shop where she and many of her friends were clients. The man was wearing a "rough-feeling" shirt, and she remembered that the suspect often wore a shirt of rough material while working. Going to the shop on a weekly basis was a social occasion, where Mother and her friends would share news and gossip and speak of personal matters. They'd never considered that their conversations could lead to danger. This man had obviously listened carefully, which would explain how he knew so much about our family, her jewelry, my father's stroke, and the fact that she was in the house alone at night. She realized he had probably watched her nightly routine from the slightly elevated street behind our house; from there he would have had a clear view of the garage and been able to observe just when she would close the door.

By the time she reached the end of this horrifying story, I was in tears of outrage and sadness for what had happened to my beloved mother. "Oh, Mother, have you called the police?" I tearfully asked.

"No."

"Aren't you going to call them?"

"No. He could find a way to hurt not only me but your father, too."

"Have you told anyone besides me?"

"I told my sister and my sister-in-law, and they agreed that it would be too dangerous to call the police."

"But if no one calls the police, he will go free and maybe try this again. Do you want me to call them?'

"No, don't you dare call them! I am not calling them either."

"Please, will you at least start closing the garage door as soon as you get out of your car and always before dark?"

"Yes, I will. Now you must promise me you won't tell your sisters."

"I promise, but are you going to be all right?"

"Yes, now stop crying. We'll talk again soon." With that, Mother hung up the phone.

I was shaking and started sobbing uncontrollably. Thirty minutes later, having pulled myself together, I broke my promise and telephoned each of my sisters. I thought they should know what had happened. They, too, broke down in tears of shock and anger. I told them of my promise and asked each one to telephone Mother as they normally did and ask how she was. I was certain she would eventually tell them, just as she had me. I suggested they might succeed in persuading her to report to the police, but they also failed in that mission.

Mother never notified the police, and neither did I or my sisters. We knew that she would be furious if we did, and we also feared that the culprit might return. She did resume her weekly appointment at the beauty shop, but not until she'd learned that her suspect had abruptly quit without giving any notice or explanation. As far as we know, no one has heard of him since. Was never calling the police a wise decision? What would you have done in similar circumstances?

Several years later we finally convinced Mother to get an alarm system—which is a whole other story.

SAME LANGUAGE, DIFFERENT ACCENT

After our mother's horrifying intrusion, my sisters and I urged her to have an alarm system installed in her house. She would never agree, until my husband, whom she adored, convinced her to do it. We were visiting her at the time, so we decided to have the system installed while we were there, lest my mother change her mind. The man from the alarm company we chose came to mother's house to explain how it would be done. He had a pronounced West Kentucky accent and kept saying that the system would be "hord ward." My husband, totally perplexed, turned to me with questioning eyes. He simply had no idea what the man was talking about. I explained that he was saying that the system would be hard wired. "Oh," said my husband, understanding at last.

When my younger sister applied for a teaching job in the state of Illinois, she was interviewed by the superintendent of that district, who was impressed with her resume, complimented her on her experience and ability, but then said, "The only thing is, you know you really have a Kentucky accent." To this she replied, "Where I come from, you're the one with the accent." She got the job.

AN ACCIDENTAL GOOD DEED,
(OR THE PORTRAIT CAPER)

By the time my father died in 1989, my sisters and I knew of his relationships with his various girlfriends—as they were euphemistically called, when in fact they were his mistresses. The relationship that lasted the longest was with a woman whom my mother always referred to as "that woman." When I no longer lived in Paducah and my middle sister was away at college, my youngest sister, who was still at home, remembers many nights when "that woman" would drive up our driveway and shine the headlights of her car into our family room, trying to see if Daddy was at home, or maybe to let him know she was tired of waiting for him to come to her. This infuriated my mother, and she would berate my father unmercifully. He would shrug and say that he couldn't help what "that woman" did.

The massive stroke my father suffered in 1980 left him paralyzed on one side and with a loss of language. He spent weeks in a nursing home before he was able to return to live in our house. During the first few weeks after the stroke, he was almost comatose. My mother went to sit with him daily. When she left at the end of the day, "that woman," who had a friend on the staff of the facility, was allowed to come in and go into my father's room. She would sit, holding his hand, until she was told to leave by other staff members.

My mother also had friends on the staff who reported these goings-on to her, which of course angered her. When we learned about it, we were angered too. We thought it brazen behavior by "that awful woman"!

Our mother died in 1998, and my sisters and I, all of whom lived away from Paducah at that point, made several trips to clean out what had been our home and decide what to keep, give away, or sell. On one of these trips, after an exhausting and emotional day, we three went out for dinner and each drank several glasses of wine. One of our quandaries was what to do with a large photographic portrait of our father, which none of us liked or wanted. Our mother had so disliked that portrait that she'd never hung or displayed it. It had stayed on the floor of our guest room closet for years, where it still resided.

When we were on our last glass of wine, my middle sister suggested we take that ugly portrait and leave it on the doorstep of "that woman." My other sister and I agreed it would be a good and revengeful prank. "But we don't know where she lives," I said.

"I do," piped up my youngest sister, who had accompanied our mother several times in the car when mother went looking for Daddy. So we went to our house, got the portrait, and drove in the dark of night to the street where she lived. We parked the car a block away from her house, turned off the headlights, and waited, to make sure no one else was around. We debated which one of us would do the deed and decided it had to be all three of us. Together we stealthily crept up to the front door, placed the portrait on the doorstep, rang the doorbell, and ran like hell back to our getaway car. We were breathlessly pleased with our naughty, revengeful caper.

Back at our house, after more giggling about our deed, we all went to bed. The upstairs telephone was in the room where I was sleeping. At around 2:00 a.m. the phone rang. I answered it, thinking it might be an emergency call from one of our kids. What I heard was a woman's quiet voice saying, "Thank you so much for the portrait. It means a lot to me." I was shocked, because I realized it was "that woman" and she was sincere. I felt foolish.

The next morning the woman who had been my mother's closest friend telephoned. Again I was the one who answered. "Did you girls leave your father's portrait on Jane's doorstep?" she questioned in an accusatory voice.

"How did you know?" I asked.

"It's all over town", she replied. It was only 8:00 a.m., and everyone in Paducah already knew of the great portrait caper! "Your mother wouldn't like that, you know," she scolded. I agreed with her and told her we were already sorry for our misdeed.

Through the years I've thought about how mistaken we were. "That woman" had really loved my father. He'd made her life better emotionally and financially. As an automobile dealer, he'd most certainly furnished her with cars. She'd owned a shop, and he might have even helped her finance the business. He'd probably assured her that he loved her and perhaps made other promises he did not intend to keep. She had grieved for him when he had the stroke. She would have known then that their life together had ended, that now he would belong totally to his family, with no room for her. She'd known she would not be welcome at his funeral or be able to grieve for him publicly. She'd truly appreciated having this large portrait of the man she had loved for many years.

What we'd instigated as a naughty prank of revenge—meant to hurt, not to comfort—had turned out to be the opposite: an appreciated good deed. We did not deserve her thanks. When I think about it now, I'm filled with guilt for not understanding at the time the depth of "that woman's" love for my father.

FRIENDS AND RELATIVES

COLLECTING STAMPS

One of my friends whom I most admired was a bubbly, funny woman, raised as a PK, or preacher's kid. She was strong in her faith but not afraid to be irreverent. When I first became acquainted with her, we were both young doctors' wives with young children. Patsy had four—three sons and a daughter, while I had two daughters. As our husbands finished their residencies and began their practices, both families moved to the same area because of its excellent school system. Our children grew up knowing each other, and Patsy and I saw each other often, both in our community and in our sorority alumnae association.

Patsy had a very busy life with her family, but she always had time to foster a baby waiting to be adopted. One never saw Patsy without a newborn in a carrier of some sort. She fostered hundreds of babies. I was quite impressed by her commitment to this program and by the fact that she made a pie for her family's dessert every single day! Imagine—a pie every day!

Patsy always had a funny story to tell, many concerning herself. My favorite was the following:

Do you remember S&H Green Stamps? They came in sheets, much like postal stamps. Various stores gave them as rewards for purchases. When a book of the stamps was filled, it could be redeemed for an item of one's choice: a toaster, a set of cookware, a blanket, or other housewares. Patsy, like almost every woman I knew, saved S&H Green Stamps and usually had some in her purse.

One day Patsy had an appointment with her gynecologist for a routine examination. When she arrived at the doctor's office, she needed to use the ladies' room before the examination. As she was doing what she went in to do, the bulb in the light fixture suddenly went out. She reached for the toilet tissue and found the roll was empty, so, in the dark, she fished around in her purse for some Kleenex to use. She then went in for her exam. Women all know what a gynecological exam entails, and I suppose most men have heard about it. When Patsy's doctor finished the exam and withdrew his rubber-gloved finger, he said, "Oh, excuse me, are you collecting these?"—as he held up several S&H Green stamps!

MEATLOAF

Aunt Jo, my aunt by marriage, made the world's worst meatloaf. I know that every cook believes that his or her meatloaf is the best, and I suppose Aunt Jo shared in that belief. She and her husband, Uncle Ralph, were both teachers and beloved by their students. Aunt Jo taught English at the junior-high level, and Uncle Ralph taught history as well as coaching the football team in the high school. They had no children of their own but became surrogate parents to many of their students, not only assisting them in their schoolwork but in many other ways. They also doted on their nieces and nephews and their children.

We were fortunate to live in the same town as Aunt Jo and Uncle Ralph, so we shared many special occasions with them. They frequently invited my husband (their nephew), me, and our two daughters to have dinner at their home. Invariably Aunt Jo made her "famous" meatloaf. It was an unappetizing color of gray and void of taste, but I threatened my daughters with their lives if they said they didn't like it, and I insisted they eat it, no matter what! Of course my husband and I did the same, so Aunt Jo believed it was our favorite. Each time we went to their home for dinner we prayed it would be anything but that wretched meatloaf. It seldom was. I could never figure out why it was so unsavory, especially when she gave me her recipe, which seemed to be foolproof. But something strange happened between the reading of and the execution of that recipe.

Years passed, and Aunt Jo and Uncle Ralph retired and moved to Sun City, Arizona. My husband and I visited them a few times, and we always insisted on taking them out for dinner, in order to avoid the dreaded meatloaf. Then Uncle Ralph died. By that time I was divorced, and my daughters were grown and following their careers. My older daughter was unable to come to the funeral in Arizona, but my younger daughter, who was living in California, was able to make the trip, so we met in the Phoenix airport. We would drive to Sun City and stay together with Aunt Jo. When we arrived at her house, Aunt Jo greeted us at the door with a tearful, "Oh, I'm so glad you're here, and I've made your favorite meatloaf." My daughter and I couldn't look at each other. When Aunt Jo showed us to the room where we would stay, closed the door, and left us to freshen up, we threw ourselves on the bed and buried our faces in the covers to smother our uncontrollable laughter. That night at dinner we again had to stifle our laughter, because our "favorite" meatloaf was as terrible tasting as ever! Perhaps somewhere along the way we should have been truthful or told her we were allergic to meatloaf. As it was, we thoroughly deceived her and certainly paid the price for our polite deception—or was it pure dishonesty?

REMEMBERING EUGENE

One of the most interesting people I've ever known was my friend Eugene Hochman, a poet and a playwright. He died in 1989 at the age of eighty-nine. He was born in Hungary, in the part we know as Transylvania, which is also known as Erdely. This area of Hungary became part of Romania at the end of WWI. It is in one of the most ancient sections of Hungary, and its natives, though now technically in Romania, always proudly pronounce themselves to be Hungarian. Eugene was no exception.

As a very young man Eugene was conscripted into the Hungarian army. The young recruits were given no training or supplies; they were just given guns and ordered to go fight. Eugene spoke of long days and nights traipsing through dense woods, with no direction, in freezing weather, with worn-out coats and boots. Worst of all, in his memory, was having to shave regularly but without razors, just broken pieces of glass. For the rest of his life he abhorred shaving, and as an elderly gentleman he shaved only every third day, planning his social life around his shaving schedule.

At the age of seventeen Eugene won the Hungarian National Poetry prize. Soon after that he had his first theatrical experience, playing the role of Hamlet in a production at the University of Prague. He was bitten by the theater bug. He began to write plays as well as act in them. He was encouraged by a teacher to emigrate to America, where his acting and playwriting would be better appreciated. His father had left Eugene's family for America in 1908, returning briefly in 1914 and then going back for good. When Eugene's teacher suggested he go to America, she asked if he didn't have relatives there. He responded that his father was "somewhere where they build automobiles." Through some sort of aid group, the teacher managed to locate Eugene's father, who sent money for him to come to America, to Detroit.

Eugene went on to earn a degree in social work at Temple University and a master's degree at the University of Michigan. Meanwhile, he was writing poetry and plays. He accumulated numerous awards, and his plays were produced in universities and theaters around the country. He was a very handsome, dramatic-looking young man, tall, with a grand manner. He claimed to be addicted to hats with brims turned down on one side, cigarette holders, and a cane.

By the time I met Eugene, he had worked many years for the board of education in Toledo, as a social worker, an educator, and a truant officer. After his beloved wife had died, he'd remarried a longtime friend of mine, Elizabeth Davies Gould, who was a well-known pianist, teacher, and composer. She and Eugene had been acquaintances in their previous marriages, and they began keeping each other company. They discovered they were soul mates. Their marriage was truly a remarkable union.

My daughters both studied piano with Elizabeth, and I became a performer of her compositions, so we were frequently in her and Eugene's company. Because they knew so many artists and interesting people, it was always stimulating to be in their home. Once one of my daughters asked me, "Why does Mr. Hochman always talk in poetry?"—for so it seemed to her. His eloquent and flowery use of the English language was magical.

Elizabeth—Teta, as she was known to her friends—and Eugene began collaborating artistically, she setting his poems to her music. They wrote an opera together called *Ray and the Gospel Singer*, and we premiered it in Toledo. Eugene became a gardener of note, encouraged by Teta, and his giant dahlias were prize winners. There was always some new interest in both their lives. When I was going through a very unhappy time in my life, I would have dinner frequently with Teta and Eugene, whose love and enthusiasm for art, beauty, and each other always lifted my spirits.

In 1987 Eugene was hospitalized several times. Once when I went to visit him there, I was alarmed as I approached his room, because several nurses, both men and women, were hovering outside his door and seemed very perturbed. I hurried to them and asked, "What's wrong? What has happened?"

"When his dinner tray was cleared Mr. Hochman kept his knife, and he refuses to give it up!" said one nurse.

"And he says he's from Transylvania!" said another.

I laughed and said, "He *is* from Transylvania, from Hungary." Apparently the only thing they knew of Transylvania was Dracula, and they were actually frightened. I told them I would go in and talk with him. "Eugene," I asked him, "why are you keeping that knife and scaring everyone?"

"Dahlink", he drawled, "I vanted a leetle *drrr-aahma!*" I loved him so much in that moment.

"Just give me the knife so that these nurses won't be afraid of you." He obeyed and reluctantly gave it to me.

As I was leaving, one of the nurses came to me and whispered, wide-eyed, "Is he really from Transylvania?" I just raised my eyebrows, shrugged my shoulders and walked on. Everyone needs a little drama now and then.

REMEMBERING BILLY

Every time I lick my lower lip, I remember Billy Draffen, the terror of my second-grade class. He was small and feisty, always itching to create mischief.

I remember thinking he was cute with his mass of dark, curly hair and twinkling eyes, but I also remember thinking of him as a troublemaker.

Our second-grade teacher, Miss Randolph, was teaching us about how the post office works. We actually made a card board façade of a post office, with a window for purchasing stamps and a slot for mailing letters. We were required to write letters, pretend to buy stamps, and mail the letters. We took turns manning the post office. Our class was seated alphabetically, so, with the last name of Woodall, I had my desk at the rear of the classroom, while Billy Draffen's was near the front. I coveted a desk on the front row.

One day, as I finished my "shift" at the post office, I was walking back to my desk when Billy stuck out his leg and tripped me. I fell right on my face, biting through my lower lip with my teeth. Blood went everywhere, and I started to cry. Miss Randolph ran to Billy, grabbed him by the collar, and rushed him to the principal's office. Then she must have attended to me or helped stop the bleeding—I don't recall. My lip started to swell, but there was no trip to the doctor. The cut left a scar, which has made Billy Draffen immortal—at least to me. I have a class photo in which I am sitting at a desk on the front row, hands clasped piously on the desk, with a very protruding lower lip and a defiant expression on my face. In this photo Billy Draffen has been relegated to the back of the room. I finally had my front-row position and my revenge!

HOMETOWN

MY HOMETOWN

My hometown of Paducah, Kentucky, located at the confluence of the Tennessee and Ohio rivers, is known as the home of Irvin S. Cobb (1876–1944), the humorist, author, and screenwriter; for being the home of the thirty-fifth Vice President of the United States, Alben W. Barkley; for the terrible flood of 1937; and for having one of the earliest Coca-Cola plants in the United States, a beautiful example of art deco architecture. It is also known for an atomic bomb plant, the National Quilt Museum, and for being home to many notable persons in the worlds of music, sports, film, and government. It has been designated by UNESCO as a Creative City of Crafts and Folk Art, which includes its unique Artist Relocation Program and Floodwall Murals. It is known for the annual Barbeque on the River Festival, where, on the last weekend of September, thirty-five or more barbeque teams compete for the title of Best Barbeque in West Kentucky. There are other edibles available, such as chicken, shrimp, tacos, funnel cakes, Cajun corn, and fried everything—from Oreos to pie, ice cream, cheesecakes, pickles, green tomatoes, and even fried BP and J's! But the star of the show is pork.

Approaching downtown Paducah during the three-day festival, one would think the entire area was on fire, there is so much smoke rising from the barbeque pits. Each team asserts that its method produces the tastiest meat and attributes the taste not only to the sauce but to the kind of wood used to smoke the meat. Hickory is the most desirable, but oak comes in as second choice. After an hour or so, the odor of all that smoking meat makes one feel a little woozy from inhaling it. The secret to tasting is to go slowly, trying just small portions at a time and approaching the sauces carefully, for they are all quite piquant. Some would call that an understatement!

Everyone in Paducah loves the Barbeque Festival, even if they don't like to eat barbeque—I've never met a Paducahan who didn't like it. In fact, when former Paducahans return home for a visit, the first place they go is Starnes Barbeque, for the taste they have missed in other parts of the country. The festival is the place to see and be seen, gather with friends, gossip, and swap tales of previous festivals. The festival itself is free, so you only pay for what you eat, and all the money raised goes to nonprofit charities in the area.

Most of the class reunions of the high schools, public and parochial, now take place during the festival, with tents set up on the lawn of the National Quilt Museum and picnic tables scattered throughout the downtown area. The fun is that one sees friends from several classes, not just one's own.

Paducah has an interesting history. It was first laid out by William Clark, of Lewis and Clark fame. It was said to be named for a Chickasaw Chief Paduke, and in fact there is a statue of Chief Paduke marking the highest spot of the 1937 floodwaters. However, authorities on the Chickasaw tribe have said there never was a chief by that name, and it was probably named for the Comanche people, known at the time as the Padoucas. Native Paducahans prefer the myth of Chief Paduke.

Paducah was host to Civil War battles and became an enormous railroad and river transportation center, on which its economy depended. It had a long period of segregated schools and clubs but never any racial hatred or violence. Desegregation came easily and smoothly. There was never any religious intolerance or prejudice either. Everyone seemed respectful of others' religious beliefs. When the Jewish synagogue was almost destroyed by fire, its congregation was welcomed to use the Methodist Church, across the street, for its services. When the Methodist Church's sanctuary was being refurbished, the Jewish people offered the sanctuary of their synagogue for use by the Methodists. Each congregation learned about the other from this experience and gained even more respect for one another.

A Jewish woman friend of mine was once chair of the pork barbeque festival. As someone said, "Only in Paducah could that happen!" This makes me proud of my hometown.

Paducah was immortalized in a song by that name in the 1943 musical *The Gang's All Here*, in which Benny Goodman played and sang, and Carmen Miranda sang and danced. The word *Paducah* seemed to go with Miranda's idea of Latin music. "Paducah, Paducah, eef you wanna you can rhyme eet with Bazooka. But you can't pooh Paducah; eet's another word for Paradise. Paducah, Paducah, just a 'preety leetle ceety in Kentucky' [as she sang it], but to me eet rhymes with lucky, when I'm looking into two blue eyes."

One of my uncles loved this song so much that he carried the words in his pocket at all times.

Paducah, my hometown, really is a pretty little city in Kentucky.

HOLLYWOOD COMES TO PADUCAH

A movie star was staying in our house—and I was missing it because I was away at college! I was so disappointed and felt thoroughly cheated.

Sometime in 1956, my father, a Ford automobile dealer, sold a car to TV and movie celebrity John Russell. He was the star of the TV series *Soldiers of Fortune* and later, his most famous role, the *Lawman* in the TV series of the same name. He also appeared in many movies. He was tall (six foot three), dark, and handsome, with large, seductive brown eyes. My father had met him when they were seat-mates on an airplane. They had begun to converse, and when John Russell had learned that my father owned a Ford dealership in Paducah, he'd expressed a desire to own "that new Thunderbird convertible." Being a consummate salesman and recognizing the possibility for invaluable publicity, my father proposed that if Mr. Russell would come to Paducah, he could have his Thunderbird at cost. Mr. Russell accepted the proposal!

A few weeks later, John Russell arrived in Paducah to take ownership of his brand-new, bright-red Thunderbird convertible. Such excitement! Not only did he arrive for his car, but he stayed in our home. Just imagine, a TV star sleeping in our guest room and having dinner in our dining room, and I was missing this wondrous happening. My younger sisters were then in elementary and junior-high school. They asked Mr. Russell if he would come to their respective classrooms so their classmates could meet him, and he did! He went to their schools and spoke and signed autographs. My sisters felt so important, and I was so envious. At my father's dealership there was much excitement, and people suddenly felt the urge to shop for a new car. Of course, they had really come to see John Russell, who posed for pictures and signed autographs. Photographs of him in his new red Thunderbird convertible were in the local newspaper and on the TV station. I telephoned home often to hear about it and read my parents' letters over and over, which were full of details.

My longed-for opportunity to meet John Russell finally took place. In August of that year my father was a delegate to the Republican convention held in San Francisco. He decided we would take a family trip before the convention began, starting in Los Angeles and then driving up the coast to San Francisco. Mr. Russell knew of our plans, and he invited my whole family to come for dinner in his home while we were there. We were thrilled, and expected to see all the Hollywood glamour we had heard of.

My sisters and I envisioned being welcomed into a gorgeous mansion by handsome Mr. Russell and his sure-to-be-beautiful and glamorous wife. We were disappointed when we arrived at a low, ranch-style house, with no manicured lawn, just ground cover that looked like kudzu to us. The house was in a neighborhood of similar ranch-style homes with the same ground cover. We think we remember it was in an area called Laurel Canyon, which is *not* Beverly Hills and is several miles away from Hollywood.

Not only were we not in palatial surroundings, but Mrs. Russell was not glamorous at all! She was tall and thin, with plain features and straight, stringy, not-quite-blonde hair. She was dressed in ordinary slacks and a simple shirt, with no diamonds, pearls, or haute couture of any sort. She "didn't match", as my sister said, the handsome, movie-star looks of her husband. She was very gracious and welcoming, and we were surprised that she had prepared the dinner herself; there was no maid or butler in sight. She was just like many Paducah wives! Our conversation, like that of ordinary people, covered many subjects, including the political convention we were soon to attend, the weather, and travel. Even without the expected glamour, it was a magical evening, and we were all thrilled. Just think—we, the Woodall family from Paducah, Kentucky, were being entertained in a movie and TV star's home!

Many years later, when I told this story to some Hollywood "insiders," they agreed it was most unusual then, and would be unheard of now, for a star to travel to a small town like ours to purchase a car and then to be so gracious and hospitable as to invite plain, ordinary folks like us into his home.

This is such a lovely memory for my entire family, and it's such fun to recall it!

SPEEDY

I've written about my hometown of Paducah and mentioned its attributes, history, and some of its famous citizens and events. But I've neglected to mention one of Paducah's most legendary figures, who was known as Speedy. His real name was Charles Atkins, and he was born in 1875 in Tennessee. At some point in his life he moved to Paducah, where he worked in a tobacco factory, baling tobacco. He earned his nickname, Speedy, because he could bale tobacco so quickly. He was an African American, poor, and without family. He drowned while fishing in the Ohio River. Speedy had become friends with A. Z. Hamock, the only Africa American undertaker in Paducah, so when Speedy's body was found, it was taken to Mr. Hamock's funeral home.

Mr. Hamock had invented a powerful preservative, and he decided to experiment with it on Speedy's corpse. The preservative worked. Speedy's skin turned a reddish brown, but his facial features were recognizable. Mr. Hamock stored Speedy in a closet and sometimes put him on display. During Paducah's great flood of 1937, Speedy's body floated away, but it was found and returned to Mr. Hamock, who reinstalled Speedy in his closet. Mr. Hamock died in 1949, and his wife then took custody of Speedy. She kept him for another forty-five years and also displayed him from time to time. If she knew Mr. Hamock's secret formula, she never told or gave it to anyone.

I was never privileged to meet Speedy, but my youngest sister did. Once when he was on view, my mother took her to see this amazing preservation specimen. My sister said that he was standing upright in the closet. His skin was mummified, but his facial features were intact. He appeared as though he could greet his visitors.

Speedy was finally given a funeral and buried in 1994 in Maple Lawn Cemetery, the oldest cemetery in Paducah. (It's where my parents and relatives are also buried.) About two hundred people attended Speedy's funeral.

I will always regret never having met Charles Atkins, our Speedy, one of the most legendary figures of my hometown's history.

A MACABRE QUESTION

Barbequed pork is one of the most-consumed foods in my hometown. There is even a Barbeque Festival on the River each September, with competitions for the best barbeque. During this festival the smoke rising from the many barbeque stands makes the downtown appear to be on fire. High school class reunions are now always held at the time of the festival. Classes have tents where they can gather, eat barbeque sandwiches, and visit. Some of the tents are on the lawn of the National Quilt Museum, another of Paducah's tourist attractions.

The flavor of barbeque differs, not only according to the sauce but also to the age and kind of wood used in the fires. My favorite barbeque comes from Starnes Barbeque, which has been in business for as long as I can remember. It was even featured on NBC's *Today* show a few years ago. Whenever I go to Paducah, I always bring Starnes barbeque home with me. This is all to set the stage for the following story.

My mother died in 1998, and I was grief-stricken. My husband, Nick, and I were with her when she was hospitalized, and she had been improving, so it was a shock when she died. My youngest sister, who lived about an hour and a half's drive from Paducah, came to help me make the arrangements with the funeral home we had used when my father had died. In fact, all my Paducah relatives had been buried by this funeral home, which had been owned by the same family for years. My sister informed me that "our" funeral home had been sold and was under new management, but they were reputed to be as caring and cooperative as the previous owners.

Nick, my sister, and I met with the new funeral director and made all the arrangements. As we were leaving, the director's assistant came up to me and asked, "Would you like a shoulder?" He thrust a large, square cardboard box in my direction.

"What?" I said, horrified at such a macabre question. "Would you like a shoulder to take home?" he repeated. Nick had the same horrified reaction as I did. We looked at each other, speechless. Then my sister started to laugh. She explained that the new owners of the funeral home, as a PR promotion, had been giving away barbequed pork shoulders, knowing that after a funeral people would be gathering at a reception, where barbeque would, of course, be served! Still looking at the assistant with some confusion, I accepted the shoulder. It was much appreciated at the gathering of family and friends after the funeral. It did provide some levity in the midst of a time of loss and grief. It has been seventeen years since that incident, and we laugh about it now, but I've often wondered how many grieving people, unaware of that promotion, were as horrified as we were by the offer of a shoulder!

Memories are wondrous gifts given to us by the people we love and admire—so that we become not just *anybody* but *somebody* special through those memories.

Printed in the United States
By Bookmasters